# TWENTIETH CENTURY VIEWS

The aim of this series is to present the best in contemporary critical opinion on major authors, providing a twentieth century perspective on their changing status in an era of profound revaluation.

Maynard Mack, *Series Editor*
Yale University

# HENRY JAMES

## A COLLECTION OF CRITICAL ESSAYS

Edited by

*Leon Edel*

Prentice-Hall, Inc., *Englewood Cliffs, N.J.*

Current printing (last digit):
12 11 10 9 8 7 6 5

LIBRARY OF CONGRESS CATALOG CARD NO.: 63-20365

*Printed in the United States of America*

C

# Table of Contents

# Introduction

*by Leon Edel*

"I seek an image, not a book," wrote Yeats. Critics, unlike poets, seek the book, but they invariably find an image. Lacking the countenance, they consciously or unconsciously fix an imaginary countenance in their mind's eye, until in the end there are as many images as there are critics, and the total image, by a process of accretion, becomes a monstrosity, an enormous imagined composite. Particularly strange is this image when the critics have encountered an artist of the mass and extent—and power—of Henry James. For then speculation and commentary, and continual exegesis, fashion a figure which can only be all things to all men.

To read the essays and reviews, as well as the books, devoted to James since the beginning of this century, in the attempt to discover the contemporary "view" of the man and his work, is to encounter some large and crudely built sphinx, over whom has been flung a prodigious coat of motley. James has been likened to Goethe, to Shakespeare, to Racine—and to Marivaux. He has been called a tragic visionary—and a melodramatist. A rootless expatriate, who came to write "more and more about less and less," he is also called the wisest man of his time. One critic says that he is a "magician"; but another that he was a soporific bore, enchanted with his own words. He has been a characteristic American intellectual; but he "turned his back" on America. Now he is a religious visionary and an allegorist; now a realist and a naturalist. A denizen of a "museum world," he has been described as churchless and godless; yet he is also seen as believing in the cult of the Virgin (has he not named two characters in one novel Maria and

Marie?). He is an unabashed aesthete; art is his religion—he is a pragmatist. He is a petty thief, a rummager in libraries; but he is also ill-informed, for "he knew nothing at all about the life of his time." He is passive and renunciatory, he is active and imaginative. He is devoid of ambition, for only an unconcerned youth would have written his early work; he had not reached "that racking impasse of vision which forces ambition upon a writer"—which "forced" James to write *The Golden Bowl.* A Tory, he would seem to have had liberal leanings; politically naïve, he was politically astute. But we must stop—the contradictions are everywhere, the images cancel each other, and James, like the proverbial politician, seems to favor prohibition because whiskey promotes poverty and squalor, and to oppose it because whiskey promotes good cheer and good fellowship. Even when individual works are examined, there is no agreement. We remember that the governess of "The Turn of the Screw" is brave and splendid and courageous and has great authority; but she is obsessed and haunted, sexually repressed, neurotic—in short, stark staring mad.

This will suggest the bizarre critical image of Henry James. The actual man, the palpable figure, is something else; he belongs to biography and most critics tend to prefer the critical to the biographical image. We have been closer to the Edwardian and the Georgian than to the Victorian Henry James. We still can see the aged writer who remained upon the London scene in our century and fixed his personal image in the mind of the then new generation of writers—a lumbering Johnsonian figure, compounding his wit out of benignity and irony, sitting massively at his club, "phantom with weighted motion, *grave incessu,* drinking the tone of things." So Ezra Pound was to remember, "and the old voice lifts itself weaving an endless sentence."

The old voice, like Dr. Johnson, could tell anecdotes, and create them as well; he had reached that stage of individual utterance that yields inimitable parody; and like the learned doctor he was a giver of literary doctrine, a novelist who criticized other novelists. In him the intellectual faculty and the discriminating mind lived perhaps too harmoniously with the creative imagination. His theories are a constant gloss upon his fictions. He has been, in a sense, the father of his form; and he was also the psychologist of personal relations. Small wonder that criticism has battened on him and grown obese. One needs, as has been said, a Baedeker to such a continent.

The essays here assembled, from among hundreds (overlooking entirely the debates and skirmishes and nagging explications) are hardly a Baedeker; they represent the anthologist's personal search for such writings on James as have been more measured than most, and more discerning—that have tried to see James whole, or to describe, with dispassion and seriousness, some important aspect of him, without intrusion of the critical *persona* and without special pleading and gratuitous conjecture.

During James's creative years there was never a time when he was not under discussion. And when he died there was more perceptive evaluation than later critics allowed. American criticism was colored by a single biographical fact during the years after James's death: he had, at the very edge of his grave, renounced his American citizenship. That he had remained an American during forty years of life in England seemed less significant to his countrymen than his last-minute decision; and many Americans turned upon him with a sense of outrage, as if the national consciousness and the national genius had been violated by this formal pledge to the newest of the Georges. By a logical, if irrelevant, step, criticism was led thus to the question of Henry James's expatriation.

Van Wyck Brooks placed it at the heart of his thesis; sensitive, poetic, possessed of a deep feeling for the American past and for the makers and finders of our literature, Brooks had embarked on the demonstration of America's coming-of-age. The lion in his path was Henry James. The novelist had come of age long before the literature he represented. Brooks's argument—it is by now generally known—was that James's late novels were impalpable and "difficult" because the novelist had uprooted himself. James was a failure in Brooks's eyes because he had long before ceased to take nourishment in the American soil; and to take such nourishment he should have stayed at home. Van Wyck Brooks held to this belief to the end. The persistence of James's reputation was an enigma to him and even a kind of academic conspiracy. That James's late novels constituted a veritable revolution in the novel form, which paved the way for the moderns, never seems to have occurred to Brooks; he confused experiment with weakness, and innovation with nationalism. But if his logic was flawed, he had a deep feeling for the qualities in James himself, and his recognition of the novelist's shortcomings was worthy of discussion even though he offered the wrong reasons for them.

This cannot be said of Vernon Parrington, who argued from a position similar to Brooks's and wrote prescriptive criticism. He seemed to judge all creativity not by aesthetic standards but by those of the Marxist fallacy; he believed there could only be a *littérature engagée,* one that depicted man's struggle for economic and social equality. For him there could be no acceptance of a status quo. Parrington, like Brooks, was writing in a pre-depression era, when Fabian thought, as disseminated by Shaw and Wells, colored much of criticism. There are signs of a revival of their views: how else are we to judge Maxwell Geismar's recent picture of the plot in the colleges to foist James and his "leisure-class cosmos" upon Americans? Thirty years ago such criticism came from the proletarian critics, and in the depression days James was called to account as a "decadent" along with Proust, a servant of capitalism instead of the "class war." But even the proletarians were divided: the gifted Robert Cantwell pointed out that James's techniques of fiction had lessons for the socially conscious novel: that a strike, depicted through a Jamesian "central intelligence"—say that of a perceptive strike leader—could have more didactic function than if depicted through the eyes of the baffled and defeated worker. As usual, James was being "used" to advance doctrinaire positions instead of being seen for his intrinsic values and his transcendent humanism.

*Autres temps, autres moeurs.* The Hitler-Stalin pact at one blow undermined prescriptive criticism in our midst and suddenly James was seen in a new light; he was no longer a rootless, effete being, he was part of the American tradition. Certain critics acknowledged that to have dismissed him on Marxist criteria, or to have used him to serve such criteria, was not to have dealt with him at all. It will perhaps suggest the flavor of these wayward years, that is of the Twenties and Thirties, if we remind ourselves that in so respected a work as *The Rise of American Civilization*

Charles and Mary Beard could depict James as using "the crude, rising bourgeoisie of America to emphasize the prettiness of the English landed aristocracy which had subdued even its latest cotton-spinning recruits to some accord with manorial taste." And the Beards also remarked that James spoke for "the poignant middle class of seasoned families, equally distressed by the doings of the plutocrats and the vulgarisms of democracy." No one reading James's tales today would deliver such a judgment: he would discover on the contrary how much James questioned the prettiness of the landed aristocracy and its manners, even as he mocked Mr. Miller of Schenectady, Mr. Gunton of Poughkeepsie, and the "money-madness" of the new skyscrapers. But even to say this is to be led into irrelevancy.

In 1943, the centenary year of Henry James, there began what has come to be called a "revival" of his work and the growth of his reputation. The word *revival* is misleading, for what had occurred was simply the slow and pervasive assertion by an American literary master of his claim to wider recognition and to a peculiar distinction as the one artistic "case" in our annals. Exception might be made for Walt Whitman, who assumed his role as poet and was never deflected from it; he took himself and his art seriously and in the end made the world take him seriously as well. This was what James did for himself as a novelist; but where Whitman proceeded from intuition James proceeded from conscious dictate and from an extraordinary dedication. The other writers of American fiction had embraced novel writing more or less by accident, and Poe and Hawthorne had perfected the short story rather than the novel; Melville stumbled into literature from his whaling ship and created an inspired and epical work. Henry James moved in another world: that of the man who from the first decided to be exclusively the artist and prepared himself carefully for that career. Fortunate in the circumstances of his childhood and family—which might have made a dilettante of him—he chose the discipline of creation; and when he could not find his peers at home, he went in search of them abroad. His expatriation, his closeness to the literary movements of his time, his insight into the way in which the race creates an imaginative whole, and his belief that the imagination knows more than the life of the time can teach it, gave him his unique place in American and world literature. The essays here gathered show that he was not neglected after his death, even though so curmudgeonery a spirit as Ezra Pound championed him as if he were Joyce or Eliot, whose battles for fame still had to be fought. Joseph Warren Beach's classic study of James's method appeared in 1918. James's letters were published in 1920; Brooks's *Pilgrimage of Henry James* and Pelham Edgar's *Henry James: Man and Author* were published during the same decade; my studies of James's playwriting phase and of his prefaces appeared in 1932; the *Hound & Horn* issue devoted to the novelist was of 1934. Edith Wharton was still writing about James just before her death in 1937; Ralph Barton Perry produced his two-volume life of William James filled with documents about the novelist in the middle of the 1930's; Edna Kenton was making her bibliographical discoveries to enlarge those of Le Roy Phillips during this time; and Edmund Wilson never lost sight of James's importance from his student years at Princeton to the present. R. P. Blackmur, the ubiquitous critic of the little magazines, assembled James's prefaces in a single volume during 1934 and was already fashioning the baroque figure of James which is his peculiar creation. We must accordingly recognize that there was in reality no "battle" for James and no "question" of James save the old one —that of espousing an artist in the face of the Philistines. The task was really one of bringing him into sharper focus and of attempting to see him "whole" rather than in the fragmentary fashion in which he was being viewed. In the 1940's, in the midst of the war, his centenary was marked not only in the better journals but also in the daily press. To be sure, publishers were slow to reprint him; and in 1942 when I broached the idea to Maxwell Perkins at Scribner's of reassembling some of the tales for the centenary, that astute editor assured me that James was thoroughly "dead" in the market place. Today, two decades later, Scribner's is reprinting the twenty-four volumes of James's "New York Edition" and Lippincott is issuing James's complete tales. If there was a "revival" it was not in criticism so much as in James's re-entry into the market place. Philip Rahv's omnibus of James's stories ushered in the new publishing era; and Clifton Fadiman, who had tended to see James earlier as an impossible mandarin of American letters, now changed his mind, and enthusiastically edited a collection of his tales. What began as a flurry in the market place was prelude to the avalanche that has come with the paperbacks.

At the time of the centenary, Henry James's executor presented to Harvard a trunkful of the novelist's papers and the voluminous family correspondence. This archive had been available to Ralph Barton Perry when he was writing *The Thought and Character of William James* and to certain other scholars. I had found in the trunk the fat "scribblers" which constituted James's notebooks as far back as 1936. I believe it was Kenneth Murdock who drew F. O. Matthiessen's attention to them, when they came to Harvard, and it was the reading of these which determined Matthiessen on his brief and busy excursion into James. A critic and explicator of poetry rather than of fiction (as the permanence of his book on T. S. Eliot shows), he plunged into a type of scholarship which involved him with literary history as much as with criticism. He worked through the archive I think with a certain impatience, recognizing in James a kindred spirit in the aesthetic world, but feeling also an estrangement from him, for Matthiessen was too much a rebel to be at ease with a novelist who took the world as he found it. His criticism of James consequently seems to me to suffer from an irrelevant use of the historical materials that came to his hand; and his use of the historical materials in turn suffered from the irrelevant use of criticism in their editing. There was a kind of displacement of effort in both directions. The greatest value of his Alexander lectures, *The Major Phase,* his anthology, *The James Family,* and his edition of certain of James's tales and novels was his insistence on the moral force of James's work and his equal insistence that James be taken seriously by an American criticism that had dealt with the novelist in too idiosyncratic and frivolous a fashion. Criticism has accepted Matthiessen's thesis that the final novels represent the summit of James's achievement; but, in justice to such predecessors as Percy Lubbock and Dorothy M. Hoare, it must be said that this claim had been made long before. His editing of the *Notebooks* with Professor Murdock placed all readers of James in their debt. Yet here too there was confusion of the critical with the editorial—and it takes great indulgence to accept Matthiessen's view that "the interest of the notebooks is not primarily historical or biographical." The word *primarily* suggests the editor's critical bias; and it is designed perhaps to cover his failure to discharge those editorial responsibilities one asks of a scholar dealing with a great document that has both historical and critical value. Matthiessen's Jamesian criticism will be read, I think, for the energy he displayed and the sensitivity he brought to a literary text. But one has only to read certain essays from other hands during the 1930's to recognize that his significance lay not so much in his insights into James as in his having advanced them and the views of his predecessors at the propitious moment in James's rising reputation.

The 1950's brought a great change in Jamesian criticism. At the end of the 1940's there had appeared Simon Nowell-Smith's witty collection of anecdotes, *The Legend of the Master,* with their penetrating analysis of how legends are created. F. W. Dupee drew upon this for his lively critical study of James written for the American Men of Letters series. This small volume served for almost a decade as an easy and lucid résumé of the then-known facts of James's career and a discussion of the principal works. Too brief to be a vade mecum, it filled that role in the absence of a larger and more systematic study. It had been preceded by Dupee's anthology, *The Question of Henry James,* a volume analogous to this one. The anthology demonstrated not so much that there was a "question" as that James had never really ceased to be a subject of discussion and speculation. The most puzzling work of the decade came also from Morningside Heights: it was an excursion into the high-fanciful posing as erudition. Written by Quentin Anderson, it sought to make of James an allegorist and a Swedenborgian, an acolyte of his father. Anderson neither offered historical evidence nor utilized traditional scholarly method. His work belongs to those recurrent speculations by which Bacon becomes Shakespeare or ciphers are discovered conveying the Bard's hidden messages to posterity. Anderson conceived of James's final novels as constituting a "trilogy" and a "divine novel" embodying the elder Henry James's religious beliefs. He boasted in his preface that he had "given the novelist a father and a past" forgetting perhaps that the novelist himself had written *Notes of a Son and Brother.*

That James used religious symbols in his works everyone knows;

they are there, the signs and emblems of the fabric of civilization out of which the novelist built his last novels. However, James was by nature a realist of the school of Balzac; and late in life, rereading Balzac, he discovered what he had earlier overlooked: that if the people and places were real in Balzac's work, the actions in which he engaged them were pure imaginings of the most romantic sort. James, in the end, himself became this kind of romantic-realist: one who believed above all in the reality of his imaginings. He held allegory in particularly low esteem. Anderson's book, however, seeks to read into each of the late novels a religious allegory with a minuteness that flies in the face of all that we know about James's personality and his creative imagination. Anderson's thesis inaugurated in the 1950's that school of criticism which reads more *into* James than out of him, and this has been true of the attempts to discover a Garden of Eden archetype in "The Turn of the Screw," a "night journey" in *The Ambassadors,* or ambiguity in narrators who reveal themselves with crystal clarity in their narratives. The consequence has been a state of anarchy in Jamesian studies, particularly in the universities.

I have in the present anthology turned away from the excesses of the criticism described above. There remain many excellent essays, more than can be included in a single book. Some measure of choice has imposed itself, and I have not used Zabel or Blackmur, Trilling or Kazin, because their writings on James have been more widely disseminated than certain others printed here. I have disregarded Mr. Leavis because I find him too opinionated and too autocratic; criticism is least useful when it is practiced as dogma. I have also avoided the source-hunting studies, this being a form of speculation least relevant when we deal with an imagination as creative as James's, an imagination so saturated with literature that all the writings of the past may be said to have provided the soil for his own work.

I have felt, however, that place should be made for Van Wyck Brooks's point of view, since it was a primary issue in the history of Jamesian criticism. To have quoted from his book on James would have been to do him an injustice; happily, in his memoirs, he summarized his position in a few admirable pages. I have used these, and it seemed logical to reprint beside them Edmund Wilson's review of Brooks in the 1920's. This illustrates not only the way in which the Brooksian arguments were met at the time, but the touchstones Mr. Wilson used then and has continued to use with a stability and maturity rare in American criticism. What strikes me most as I survey the essays are those of the 1930's which were being written even when the Marxists pre-empted the foreground. Some of the best essays in this volume are of that period; they were not only the best answer to the Marxists, but they show that even before the so-called "revival" a very full measure of James had been taken: indeed, in spite of our saturated American studies, we have had nothing quite so good as the work of these earlier critics.

For the rest, I have not thought it useful to include any examples of the leftist criticism, which reads curiously today and is better buried with the ephemera of its time. Nor are there examples of the exegetes and the allegory seekers, since these tell us less about James than about the critics themselves. I have sought, in other words, those critiques which are general and broad, illustrative and "basic." For the rest I can only plead individual preference or individual bias. These are always the prerogative of the anthologist.

# An Appreciation

## *by Joseph Conrad*

The critical faculty hesitates before the magnitude of Mr. Henry James's work. His books stand on my shelves in a place whose accessibility proclaims the habit of frequent communion. But not all his books. There is no collected edition to date, such as some of "our masters" have been provided with; no neat row of volumes in buckram or half-calf putting forth a hasty claim to completeness, and conveying to my mind a hint of finality, of a surrender to fate of that field in which all these victories have been won. Nothing of the sort has been done for Mr. Henry James's victories in England.*

In a world such as ours, so painful with all sorts of wonders, one would not exhaust oneself in barren marveling over mere bindings, had not the fact, or rather the absence of the material fact, prominent in the case of other men whose writing counts (for good or evil)—had it not been, I say, expressive of a direct truth spiritual and intellectual; an accident of—I suppose—publishing business acquiring a symbolic meaning from its negative nature. Because, emphatically, in the body of Mr. Henry James's work there is no suggestion of finality, nowhere a hint of surrender, or even of mere probability of surrender, to his own victorious achievement in that field where he is master. Happily, he will never be able to claim completeness; and, were he to confess to it in a mo-

"An Appreciation." (Originally entitled "Henry James: An Appreciation.") From *Notes on Life and Letters* (London: J. M. Dent & Sons, 1905) by Joseph Conrad, pp. 13-23. 

* This was written two years before the appearance of the "New York Edition" of James's novels and tales in twenty-four volumes. [Ed. Note.]

ment of self-ignorance, he would not be believed by the very minds for whom such a confession naturally would be meant. It is impossible to think of Mr. Henry James becoming "complete" otherwise than by the brutality of our common fate whose finality is meaningless—in the sense of its logic being of a material order, the logic of a falling stone.

I do not know into what brand of ink Mr. Henry James dips his pen; indeed, I heard that of late he has been dictating; but I know that his mind is steeped in the waters flowing from the fountain of intellectual youth. The thing—a privilege—a miracle—what you will—is not quite hidden from the meanest of us who run as we read. To those who have the grace to stay their feet it is manifest. After some twenty years of attentive acquaintance with Mr. Henry James's work, it grows into absolute conviction, which, all personal feeling apart, brings a sense of happiness into one's artistic existence. If gratitude, as some one defined it, is a lively sense of favors to come, it becomes very easy to be grateful to the author of *The Ambassadors*—to name the latest of his works. The favors are sure to come; the spring of *that* benevolence will never dry up. The stream of inspiration runs brimful in a predetermined direction, unaffected by the periods of drought, untroubled in its clearness by the storms of the land of letters, without languor or violence in its force, never running back upon itself, opening new visions at every turn of its course through that richly inhabited country its fertility has created for our delectation, for our judgment, for our exploring. It is, in fact, a magic spring.

With this phrase the metaphor of the perennial spring, of the inextinguishable youth, of running water, as applied to Mr. Henry James's inspiration, may be dropped. In its volume and force the body of his work may be compared rather to a majestic river. All creative art is magic, is evocation of the unseen in forms persuasive, enlightening, familiar and surprising, for the edification of mankind, pinned down by the conditions of its existence to the earnest consideration of the most insignificant tides of reality.

Action in its essence, the creative art of a writer of fiction may be compared to rescue work carried out in darkness against cross gusts of wind swaying the action of a great multitude. It is rescue work, this snatching of vanishing phases of turbulence, disguised in fair words, out of the native obscurity into a light where the struggling forms may be seen, seized upon, endowed with the only possible form of permanence in this world of relative values—the permanence of memory. And the multitude feels it obscurely too; since the demand of the individual to the artist is, in effect, the cry, "Take me out of myself!" meaning, really, out of my perishable activity into the light of imperishable consciousness. But everything is relative, and the light of consciousness is only enduring, merely the most enduring of the things of this earth, imperishable only as against the short-lived work of our industrious hands.

When the last aqueduct shall have crumbled to pieces, the last air-ship fallen to the ground, the last blade of grass shall have died upon a dying earth, man, indomitable by his training in his resistance to misery and pain, shall set this undiminished light of his eyes against the feeble glow of the sun. The artistic faculty, of which each of us has a minute grain, may find its voice in some individual of that last group, gifted with a power of expression, and courageous enough to interpret the ultimate experience of mankind in terms of his temperament, in terms of art. I do not mean to say that he would attempt to beguile the last moments of humanity by an ingenious tale. It would be too much to expect —from humanity. I doubt the heroism of the hearers. As to the heroism of the artist, no doubt is necessary. There would be on his part no heroism. The artist in his calling of interpreter creates (the clearest form of demonstration) because he must. He is so much of a voice that for him silence is like death; and the postulate was that there is a group alive, clustered on his threshold to watch the last flicker of light on a black sky, to hear the last word uttered in the stilled workshop of the earth. It is safe to affirm that, if anybody, it will be the imaginative man who would be moved to speak on the eve of that day without tomorrow—whether in austere exhortation or in a phrase of sardonic comment, who can guess?

For my own part, from a short and cursory acquaintance with my kind, I am inclined to think that the last utterance will formulate, strange as it may appear, some hope now to us utterly inconceivable. For mankind is delightful in its pride, its assurance, and its indomitable tenacity. It will sleep on the battlefield among its own dead, in the manner of an army having won a barren victory. It will not know when it is beaten. And, perhaps, it is right in that quality. The victories are not, perhaps, so barren as it may appear from a purely strategical, utilitarian point of view. Mr. Henry James seems to hold that belief. Nobody has rendered better, perhaps, the tenacity of temper, or known how to drape the robe of spiritual honor about the drooping form of a victor in a barren strife. And the honor is always well won; for the struggles Mr. Henry James chronicles with such subtle and direct insight are, though only personal contests desperate in their silence, none the less heroic (in the modern sense) for the absence of shouted watch-words, clash of arms and sound of trumpets. Those are adventures in which only choice souls are ever involved. And Mr. Henry James records them with a fearless and insistent fidelity to the *péripéties* of the contest, and the feelings of the combatants.

The fiercest excitements of a romance *"de cape et d'épée,"* the romance of yard-arm and boarding-pike so dear to youth, whose knowledge of action (as of other things) is imperfect and limited, are matched, for the quickening of our maturer years, by the tasks set, by the difficulties presented, to Mr. Henry James's men's and women's sense of truth, of necessity—before all, of conduct. His mankind is delightful. It is delightful in its tenacity; it refuses to own itself beaten; it will sleep on the battlefield. These warlike images come by themselves under the pen; since, from the duality of man's nature and the competition of individuals, the life history of the earth must in the last instance be a history of a really very relentless warfare. Neither his fellows, nor his gods, nor his passions will leave a man alone. In virtue of these allies and enemies, he holds his precarious dominion, he possesses his fleeting significance; and it is this relation, in all its manifestations, great and little, superficial or profound, and this relation alone, that is commented upon, interpreted, demonstrated by the art of the novelist in the only possible way in which the task can be performed: by the independent creation of circumstance and character, achieved against all the difficulties of expression, in an imaginative effort finding its inspiration from the reality of forms and sensations. That a sacrifice must be made, that something has to be given up, is the truth engraved in the innermost recesses of the fair temple built for our edification by the masters of fiction. There is no other secret behind the curtain. All adventure, all love, every success is resumed in the supreme energy of an act of renunciation. It is the uttermost limit of our power; it is the most potent and effective force at our disposal, on which rest the labors of a solitary man in his study, the rock on which have been built commonwealths whose might casts a dwarfing shadow upon two oceans. Like a natural force which is obscured as much as illustrated by the multiplicity of phenomena, the power of renunciation is obscured by the mass of weaknesses, vacillations, secondary motives and false steps and compromises which make up the sum of our activity. But no man or woman worthy of the name can pretend to anything more, to anything greater. And Mr. Henry James's men and women are worthy of the name, within the limits his art, so clear, so sure of itself, has drawn round their activities. He would be the last to claim for them Titanic proportions. The earth itself has grown smaller in the course of ages. But in every sphere of human perplexities and emotions there are more greatnesses than one—not counting here the greatness of the artist himself. Wherever he stands, at the beginning or the end of things, a man has to sacrifice his gods to his passions or his passions to his gods. That is the problem, great enough, in all truth, if approached in the spirit of sincerity and knowledge.

In one of his critical studies, published some fifteen years ago, Mr. Henry James claims for the novelist the standing of the historian as the only adequate one, as for himself and before his audience. I think that the claim cannot be contested, and that the position is unassailable. Fiction is history, human history, or it is nothing. But it is also more than that; it stands on firmer ground, being based on the reality of forms and the observation of social phenomena, whereas history is based on documents and the reading of print and handwriting—on second-hand impression. Thus fiction is nearer truth. But let that pass. A historian may be an artist too, and a novelist is a historian, the preserver, the keeper, the expounder, of human experience. As is meet for a man of his descent and tradition, Mr. Henry James is the historian of fine consciences.

Of course, this is a general statement; but I don't think its truth will be or can be questioned. Its fault is that it leaves so much out;

and, besides, Mr. Henry James is much too considerable to be put into the nutshell of a phrase. The fact remains that he has made his choice, and that his choice is justified up to the hilt by the success of his art. He has taken for himself the greater part. The range of a fine conscience covers more good and evil than the range of a conscience which may be called, roughly, not fine; a conscience less troubled by the nice discrimination of shades of conduct. A fine conscience is more concerned with essentials; its triumphs are more perfect, if less profitable in a worldly sense. There is, in short, more truth in its working for a historian to detect and to show. It is a thing of infinite complication and suggestion. None of these escape the art of Mr. Henry James. He has mastered the country, his domain, not wild indeed, but full of romantic glimpses, of deep shadows and sunny places. There are no secrets left within his range. He has disclosed them as they should be disclosed—that is, beautifully. And, indeed, ugliness has but little place in this world of his creation. Yet it is always felt in the truthfulness of his art; it is there, it surrounds the scene, it presses close upon it. It is made visible, tangible, in the struggles, in the contacts of the fine consciences, in their perplexities, in the sophism of their mistakes. For a fine conscience is naturally a virtuous one. What is natural about it is just its fineness, an abiding sense of the intangible, everpresent, right. It is most visible in their ultimate triumph, in their emergence from miracle, through an energetic act of renunciation. Energetic, not violent: the distinction is wide, enormous, like that between substance and shadow.

Through it all Mr. Henry James keeps a firm hold of the substance, of what is worth having, of what is worth holding. The contrary opinion has been, if not absolutely affirmed, then at least implied, with some frequency. To most of us, living willingly in a sort of intellectual moonlight, in the faintly reflected light of truth, the shadows so firmly renounced by Mr. Henry James's men and women stand out endowed with extraordinary value, with a value so extraordinary that their rejection offends, by its uncalled-for scrupulousness, those businesslike instincts which a careful Providence has implanted in our breasts. And, apart from that just cause of discontent, it is obvious that a solution by rejection must always present a certain apparent lack of finality, especially startling when contrasted with the usual methods of solution by rewards and punishments, by crowned love, by fortune, by a broken leg or a sudden death. Why the reading public, which, as a body, has never laid upon a story-teller the command to be an artist, should demand from him this sham of Divine Omnipotence is utterly incomprehensible. But so it is; and these solutions are legitimate, inasmuch as they satisfy the desire for finality, for which our hearts yearn with a longing greater than the longing for the loaves and fishes of this earth. Perhaps the only true desire of mankind, coming thus to light in its hours of leisure, is to be set at rest. One is never set at rest by Mr. Henry James's novels. His books end as an episode in life ends. You remain with the sense of the life still going on; and even the subtle presence of the dead is felt in that silence that comes upon the artist-creation when the last word has been read. It is eminently satisfying, but it is not final. Mr. Henry James, great artist and faithful historian, never attempts the impossible.

# Jacobean and Shavian

*by Max Beerbohm*

## I
## *Mr. Shaw's* Roderick Hudson

When an artist takes a theme which has already been taken by another and very different artist, comparison of the two works is sure to amuse us, and will probably, too, instruct us, helping us to realize the peculiarities of each man more clearly than before.

One of Mr. Henry James's earliest themes was a youth endowed with artistic genius, but not endowed with moral sense. Roderick Hudson, whom you doubtless remember—for who, having read the book, could forget him?—went about "using" people quite unscrupulously, taking everything, giving nothing except his fascination, and caring not a jot how much distress he inflicted on the people around him. Louis Dubedat, the central figure of Mr. Shaw's new play,[1] is, essentially, just such another as Roderick Hudson. But Mr. Shaw is, essentially, not just such another as Mr. Henry James. Indeed I cannot imagine two minds, or two artistic methods, more divergent than the Shavian and the Jacobean. Mr. James must excuse my invention of this adjective. To Mr. Shaw I need not apologize, for "Shavian" was invented by himself. He was the first to feel the need of that adjective. He has ever been conscious of himself as a peculiar, definite, detached force—a light that must not be hidden under a bushel. Mr. James, on the other hand, has never

"Jacobean and Shavian." I. "Mr. Shaw's *Roderick Hudson,*" November 24, 1906, pp. 260-265; II. "Mr. Henry James's Play," February 27, 1909, pp. 323-326. From *Around Theatres* by Max Beerbohm. 

[1] *The Doctor's Dilemma.*

seemed to have that kind of self-consciousness (a word which I use in no derogatory sense). So far as he is conscious of self, he is eager only for self-effacement. He has used the "first person singular" very often in his stories; but only because he can observe his characters the more closely by playing some subordinate part in their midst. He is devoted, passionately, to his art—the art of portraying men and women as he sees them. He never judges men and women. Or rather, he never pronounces judgment. No industrious and intuitive reader of his books can have failed to deduce that he has a very strong moral sense. He hates selfishness. He loves honor—loves, indeed, a sense of honor so punctilious that its effects are apt to be rather exasperating to readers who are only averagely good. But he never lets his moral prejudices be prejudicial to his characters. He never tries to set in an unduly attractive light the things that he loves, or to blacken the things that he hates. The hand of the artist in him is held tightly over the mouth of the preacher. In Mr. Shaw, the preacher is ever vocal. Not that the artist in him is weak or idle: he manfully tries that all the characters shall have fair play. The preacher disapproves strongly of them, for the most part. They are all, with few exceptions, on the penitents' bench. But the artist insists that they shall all have their say, and a respectful hearing. And the ratiocinator (who is even stronger than the preacher in Mr. Shaw, and stronger far than the artist) insists that they shall all, severally, score—to the greater glory of G. B. S.

Louis Dubedat scores right and left. He is always scoring. He scores even under the shadow of death. And Mr. Shaw has, moreover, been as anxious to make his death bed pathetic as was Dickens to make Little Nell's. And, where Dickens failed, Mr. Shaw has succeeded. The pathos here is real. I defy you not to be touched by it, while it lasts. But I defy you, when it is over, to mourn. Even if the curtain fell on Dubedat's dying breath, you would feel that his death was a good riddance. In point of fact, the curtain does not fall for some time. We hear the unemotional comments of the doctors, varied by the very emotional comments of one of them. I could feel that the audience did not like this. And, though I have not, at the moment of writing, read any of the criticisms, I am sure that Mr. Shaw has been more or less violently attacked for lack of taste. Certainly the scene was rather painful. But if it was a true scene, what matter? And it *is* true that doctors do not take death emotionally. The sentimental platitudes uttered by one of the doctors in this scene would not have been uttered by him in real life, for the sole benefit of his colleagues. In that respect, the scene is untrue. But let no one suggest that these platitudes, absurd though they are, are not very like the kind of thing that would be said, at such a juncture, by a rather stupid layman. Clever people, in the midst of great emotion, say nothing; for they know that whatever they might say would be inadequate. Stupid people rush into speech, speech not one whit more ridiculous than this doctor's. No, Mr. Shaw was not merely "playing for a laugh." He was trying to reproduce a thing that exists in life. And his error was but in forgetting that this man was a doctor addressing himself to his colleagues. There was no "error of taste," such as, I am sure, he has been accused of. Nor was there an error of art. For, as I have said, we do not, after a moment, feel the slightest desire to mourn Dubedat.

And yet we have never ceased to mourn Roderick Hudson. He was a selfish brute, but he cast his spell as surely over us readers as he did over all the characters in the book. We, too, would have gladly sacrificed ourselves to his convenience. We believed in his genius. Those few things that he wrought—the Adam, the Eve, the bust of his mother, and one or two others—were as real to us and as fine as though we had beheld them with our own eyes. And when Roderick Hudson died we thought of all those blocks of marble from which beauty would never spring now. Mr. James has a wonderful way of imagining and describing works of art. He infects us with his own enthusiasm. The works of art are as real to us as they are to him. Fortunately his books are not illustrated with reproductions of some artist's notion of the masterpieces described. Such illustrations, however admirable, would tend to damp our enthusiasm. And, doubtless, one of the reasons why we do not fervently believe in the genius of Louis Dubedat is that we see his work. I do not say that they are not "able," these sketches on the walls of his studio. Evidently, Dubedat could have earned plenty of money as a "black and white man" on an illustrated weekly paper. And the posthumous "one man show" is a revelation of his versatility. Dubedat seems to have caught, in his brief lifetime, the various styles of *all* the young lions of the Carfax Gallery. Budding genius is always, I know, imitative; but not so frantically imitative as all that. Nor was Dubedat exactly a budding genius. We are asked to accept him as a soon-to-be-recognized master. Of course, it is not Mr. Shaw's fault that the proper proofs are not forthcoming. But it certainly is a fault in Mr. Shaw that he wished proper proofs to forthcome. He ought to have known that even if actual masterpieces by one unknown man could have been collected by the propertymaster, we should yet have wondered whether Dubedat was so very remarkable after all. Masterpieces of painting must be left to an audience's imagination. And Mr. Shaw's infringement of so obvious a rule is the sign of a certain radical lack of sensitiveness in matters of art. Only by suggestion can these masterpieces be made real to us. And how can this suggestion best be made to us? Clearly, by the character and conversation of the artist himself as presented on the stage, and (in a lesser degree) by what is said of his work by other persons in the play.

The other persons in the play say a good deal about Dubedat's work. Mrs. Dubedat, especially, dwells on it. But a wife's evidence is no more admissible in the case of an artist than in the case of a man charged with murder. One of the doctors is a connoisseur, and freely buys Dubedat's work. But the evidence of one connoisseur is not final. We examine Dubedat himself. He talks much, and well, about art. So do many quite bad painters. Indeed, it is generally the quite bad painters who are most fluent. Good painters think rather with their eyes and hands than with their brains, and thus have a difficulty in general conversation. If you coax them from silence, they will describe illuminatively, but they cannot ratiocinate: that is not their business. It is very much the business of Louis Dubedat. As I have said, he scores right and left. He has among strangers none of the shyness and the unreadiness of a man who can paint. And he "knocks off" brilliant sketches on the backs of menus with all the good nature of a man who can't. In a word, we disbelieve in him as a genius. Only as a scamp is he real to us.

And his very scampishness is of a kind that would destroy any illusion we might have of him as a great painter. His is not the large, vague unscrupulousness of self-centered genius. It is the "slimness" of the confidence-trick man. When I said that Dubedat was "essentially" the same as Roderick Hudson, I meant, of course, that Mr. Shaw's intention had been the same as Mr. James's. But Mr. Shaw's deep-rooted disgust for the unmoral artist has prevented him, despite his constant effort at fairness, from presenting this figure worthily. The ever-quick succession of petty impostures played by Dubedat is, of course, vastly amusing, but . . . why all these buts? Why have I been carping all this while about the central figure, instead of expressing the joy that the whole brilliant play gave me, and trying to communicate something of that joy to you? I evidently haven't yet learnt my business.

## II
### *Mr. Henry James's Play*

From Jerome to James—from *The Passing of the Third-Floor Back* to *The High Bid*—it is rather a long way for an actor to travel, is it not? And yet my first impression of Mr. Forbes-Robertson, at the Afternoon Theatre, was that he had walked literally out of the one play into the other. The last I had seen of him was his back, graciously bowed, as he passed slowly out of the front door of the Bloomsbury lodging house, with a momentary illumination in the fanlight to show that "The Stranger" was more or less divine. And now it seemed as if the stage had just been swung round on a pivot: here was the front of "The Stranger"; the tender, grave, gently radiant front; emerging, however, not into Gower Street, but into the hall of a great old house in the country. Knowing that the central man in Mr. James's play, besides having served in the Army, was an active worker in East-end settlements, and not a mere aimless rambler in Jeromian platitudes, I rather feared that he had not found an ideal representative—that he had found too idealistic a representative—in Mr. Forbes-Robertson. But my misgiving soon vanished. The actor soon threw off the sublimity of mien that was needed to make Mr. Jerome's sort of thing pass muster, and showed that for the interpretation of Mr. James's sort of thing he was exquisitely equipped. "What are you exactly?" asks Captain Yule of the aged and shabby butler who is in charge of the house; "I mean, to whom do you beautifully *belong*?" There, in those six last words, is quintessence of Mr. James; and the sound of them sent innumerable little vibrations through the heart of every good Jacobite in the audience. Mr. Walkley, properly vibrant, treasured the words up to be the refrain of a criticism for which all we fellow-Jacobites of his are grateful to him. The words could not have been more perfectly uttered than they were by Mr. Forbes-Robertson. We realized at once to whom *he* beautifully belongs. It is to Mr. Henry James. Mr. Walkley, I notice, places the word "beautifully" between two parenthetic dashes; and certainly this way of notation gives the true cadence better than the way that I have used—the way that Mr. James himself would use; but it is still very far from the perfection of Mr. Forbes-Robertson's rendering of the words. "To whom do you—beautifully *belong*?" is nearer. But how crude a medium print is—or even handwriting—for expression of what such a face and voice as Mr. Forbes-Robertson's can express! In his eyes, as he surveyed the old butler, and in his smile, and in the groping hesitancy before the adverb was found, and in the sinking of the tone at the verb, there was a whole world of good feeling, good manners, and humor. It was love seeing the fun of the thing. It was irony kneeling in awe. It was an authentic part of the soul of Mr. James.

When I think of Mr. James's books, and try to evaluate the immense delight I have had in that immense array of volumes, it seems to me that in my glow of gratitude the thing I am most of all grateful for is not the quality of the work itself, but the quality of the man revealed through that work. Greater than all my aesthetic delight in the books is my moral regard for the author. This confession, if it chance to meet his eye, may startle him. He was not in Paris in the early Seventies for nothing. His "form" in fiction rigidly forbids self-assertion. Not his to buttonhole us and tell us what he thinks of his characters. We must find out about them for ourselves. No philosophics will be expounded to us, no morals pointed for us. The author, as at the Afternoon Theatre the other day, "is not in the house." Well, this is a "form" like another. It is not, as it was thought to be, final, inevitable; it is already going out of fashion. Certainly, if illusion of reality were the sole aim of fiction, this "form" would be the only right one. Reality flies out of the window when the author comes in at the door. Nevertheless, even the most retiring author must, in the nature of things, be somewhere concealed on the premises; and you will find him if you look for him. Mr. James is devious—say, in a cupboard in the basement. But rout him out: the "find" is its own reward, and an ample one. "E. A. B." of the *Daily News* pronounces that Mr. James, whose books he had read, is "a clever man"—a remark that gives me somewhat the impulse that Charles Lamb had in regard to a gentleman who had fired off precisely that remark about Shakespeare. How much more than clever Mr. James is, how many qualities unrelated to cleverness are in him, is measured for us by the fatuous inadequacy of this remark from a man who is, as "E. A. B." is, himself a very clever man. "Subtle," adds "E. A. B.," as a make weight. It is the Gradus epithet for Mr. James, and saves time. But I am sorry for anyone who, having read even but one or two of Mr. James's earliest short stories, could find no other epithets to affix. And you need search heart and brain for epithets to describe the later James —the James who has patiently evolved a method of fiction entirely new, entirely his own, a method that will probably perish with him, since none but he, one thinks, could handle it; that amazing method by which a novel competes not with other novels, but with life itself; making people known to us as we grow to know them in real life, by hints, by glimpses, here a little and there a little, leaving us always guessing and wondering, till, in the fullness of time, all these scraps of revelation gradually resolve themselves into one large and luminous whole, just as in real life. To read (say) *The Golden Bowl* or *The Wings of the Dove* is like taking a long walk uphill, panting and perspiring and almost of a mind to turn back, until, when you look back and down, the country is magically expanded beneath your gaze, as you never saw it yet; so that you toil on gladly up the heights, for the larger prospects that will be waiting for you. I admit, you must be in good training. People often say "Oh, what a pity it is that dear Henry James won't write the sort of books he *used* to write. Do you remember *The Portrait of a Lady*?" etc., etc. I always hint to these people, as politely as possible, that an artist's business is not to keep pace with his admirers, and that their business is to keep pace, if possible, with *him;* and that, if they faint by the way, they will be safer in blaming themselves than in blaming *him.* Mr. James, that very conscious and devoted artist, may be trusted, he especially, to have followed the right line of progress— to have got the logical development of his own peculiar gifts. I know no fictionist so evidently steeped as he is in the passion for literature as a fine art—none who has taken for his theme writers and writing so often, and with such insight. "The Figure in the Carpet," "The Aspern Papers," "The Death of the Lion," "The Middle Years," "The Lesson of the Master"—where is the literary passion and conscience drawn for us so lovingly, and analyzed so cunningly, as in these grand short stories by this master? That his sense of beauty is not confined to the manifestations of art in letters, that he has a passionate eye for what is fine in the arts of sculpture and painting and architecture, and for what is fine in Nature, is very manifest to all readers of him in his early and middle periods. And sometimes I cannot help regretting that in his present period he vouchsafes us none of those extraordinarily sensitive visual impressions that were so integral a feature of his tales. Gradually, austerely, they have been banished, these impressions of his, by force of that greater passion of insight into the souls of men and women. I had nearly written of "ladies and gentlemen." For it is very true that Mr. James does not deal with raw humanity, primitive emotions and so on. Civilization, and a high state of it at that, is the indispensable milieu for him; and just when the primitive emotions surge up in the complex bosoms of his creatures, to cause an explosion, Mr. James escapes with us under his wing, and does not lead us back until the crisis is over—until the results, the to him so much more interesting results, may be quietly examined. I suppose it is by reason of his avoidance of emotional crisis even in the most complex bosoms, that Mr. James has so often been charged with lack of human feeling. Well, there are all sorts of human feelings; they aren't all summed up in *Antony and Cleopatra,* there are plenty of them left over; and Mr. James's characters are made to display a very full share. The feeling that they display most constantly is the feeling for right and wrong, for what is noble in conduct and what ignoble. It is by this that they are especially preoccupied, whether or not their conduct be—it usually is—thereby conditioned. The passion of conscience, a sort of lyrical conscience, conscience raised to the pitch of ecstasy, both in great matters and in small, is what is so common among Mr. James's characters that one might almost take it as a common denominator. When you find the creatures of a creative artist animated thus by one recurring motive, you need not be a skilled detective to "spot" the main characteristic of that artist as man. Despite his resolute self-suppression for his "form's" sake, Mr. Henry James, through his books, stands out as clearly to me as any preacher I have seen perched up in a pulpit. And I do not happen to have heard any preacher in whom was a moral fervor so great as (with all its restraint) is Mr. James's fervor, or one whose outlook on the world seemed to me so fine and touching and inspiring, so full of reverence for noble things and horror of things ignoble—a horror and a reverence that are never obscured for me by the irony that is so often Mr. James's way of writing. More perfectly, perhaps, than in any other work of his do we find expressed in that dear masterpiece "The Altar of the Dead" the—but I am coming to the end of my "space," and have done so very little to justify the title of my article.

My excuse must be that of all that I love in Mr. James's mind so very little can be translated into the sphere of drama. I well remember reading *The High Bid* in the volume entitled *The Two Magics*; and it was clear to me that the story had been conceived (and perhaps written) as a play and then wrought into narrative form. The arrangement of entrances and exits was proof enough of that. But further proof was in the trite conventionality of the story—precisely the sort of story that a true man of letters would select for a venture in dramaturgy, muttering, "I suppose this is the sort of thing they understand." Needless to say, the workmanship was exquisite; and the characters, though essentially puppets, moved with a lively grace and distinction, a bright reality of surface, so that you half forgot they were unreal. What I say of the story is equally true of the play. I have spoken already of the delight it is to hear Mr. James's dialogue from the lips of Mr. Forbes-Robertson, who is not merely Captain Yule but a figure that evokes innumerable cherished memories of Mr. James's books at large—the very spirit of Jacobeanism. Mr. Ian Forbes-Robertson is fine as the old butler. And Miss Gertrude Elliott's vivacity and touching grace are just what are needed for Mrs. Gracedew. *The High Bid* is not the only story that bears traces of having been conceived by Mr. James as a play; and I hope Mr. Forbes-Robertson will soon claim the one or two others. For, little though Mr. James can on the stage give us of his great art, even that little has a quality which no other man can give us; an inalienable magic.

# A Brief Note

*by Ezra Pound*

Some may say that his work was over, well over, finely completed, and heaven knows there is mass—a monument of that work, heavy for one man's shoulders to have borne up, labor enough for two lifetimes; still we would have had a few more years of his writing. Perhaps the grasp was relaxing, perhaps we should have had no strongly planned book; but we should have had paragraphs cropping up here and there. Or we should have had, at least, conversation, wonderful conversation; and even if we did not hear it ourselves, we should have known that it was going on somewhere. The massive head, the slow uplift of the hand, *gli occhi onesti e tardi,* the long sentences piling themselves up in elaborate phrase after phrase, the lightning incision, the pauses, the slightly shaking admonitory gesture with its "wu-w-wait a little, wait a little, something will come," blague and benignity and the weight of so many years' careful, incessant labor, of minute observation always there to enrich the talk. I had heard it but seldom, yet it was all unforgettable.

The man had this curious power of founding affection in those who had scarcely seen him and even in many who had not, who but knew him at second hand.

No man who has not lived on both sides of the Atlantic can well appraise Henry James; his death marks the end of a period. The *Times* says: "The Americans will understand his changing his nationality," or something of that sort. The "Americans" will understand nothing whatsoever about it. They have undersood nothing

"A Brief Note." From *The Literary Essays of Ezra Pound. The Little Review* (August 1918), pp. 6-9. 

about it. They do not even know what they lost. They have not stopped for eight minutes to consider the meaning of his last public act. After a year of ceaseless labor, of letter writing, of argument, of striving in every way to bring in America on the side of civilization, he died of apoplexy. On the side of civilization—civilization against barbarism, civilization, not Utopia, not a country or countries where the right always prevails in six weeks! After a lifetime spent in trying to make two continents understand each other, in trying, and only his thoughful readers can have any conception of how he had tried, to make three nations intelligible one to another. I am tired of hearing pettiness talked about Henry James's style. The subject has been discussed enough in all conscience, along with the minor James. What I have not heard is any word of the major James, of the hater of tyranny; book after early book against oppression, against all the sordid petty personal crushing oppression, the domination of modern life, not worked out in the diagrams of Greek tragedy, not labeled "epos" or "Aeschylus." The outbursts in *The Tragic Muse,* the whole of "The Turn of the Screw," human liberty, personal liberty, the rights of the individual against all sorts of intangible bondage! [1] The passion of it, the continual passion of it in this man who, fools said, didn't "feel." I have never yet found a man of emotion against whom idiots didn't raise this cry.

And the great labor, this labor of translation, of making America intelligible, of making it possible for individuals to meet across national borders. I think half the American idiom is recorded in Henry James's writing, and whole decades of American life that otherwise would have been utterly lost, wasted, rotting in the unhermetic jars of bad writing, of inaccurate writing. No English reader will ever know how good are his New York and his New England; no one who does not see his grandmother's friends in the pages of the American books. The whole great assaying and weigh-

[1] This holds, despite anything that may be said of his fuss about social order, social tone. I naturally do not drag in political connotations, from which H. J. was, we believe, wholly exempt. What he fights is "influence," the impinging of family pressure, the impinging of one personality on another; all of them in highest degree damn'd, loathsome, and detestable. Respect for the peripheries of the individual may be, however, a discovery of our generation; I doubt it, but it seems to have been at low ebb in some districts (not rural) for some time.

ing, the research for the significance of nationality, French, English, American. No one seems to talk of these things.

"An extraordinary old woman, one of the few people who is really doing anything good." There were the cobwebs about connoisseurship, etc., but what do they matter? Some yokel writes in the village paper, as Henley had written before, "James's stuff was not worth doing." Henley has gone pretty completely. America has not yet realized that never in history has one of her great men abandoned his citizenship out of shame. It was the last act—the last thing left. He had worked all his life for the nation and for a year he had labored for the national honor. No other American was of sufficient importance for his change of allegiance to have constituted an international act; no other American would have been welcome in the same public manner. America passes over these things, but the thoughtful cannot pass over them.

Armageddon, the conflict? I turn to James's "A Bundle of Letters"; a letter from "Dr. Rudolph Staub" in Paris, ending:

> You will, I think, hold me warranted in believing that, between precipitate decay and internecine enmities, the English-speaking family is destined to consume itself and that with its decline the prospect of general pervasiveness, to which I alluded above, will brighten for the deep-lunged children of the Fatherland!

We have heard a great deal of this sort of thing since; it sounds very natural. My edition of the volume containing these letters was printed in '83, and the imaginary letters were written somewhat before that. I do not know that this calls for comment. Henry James's perception came thirty years before Armageddon. That is all I wish to point out. Flaubert said of the War of 1870: "If they had read my *Education Sentimentale,* this sort of thing wouldn't have happened." Artists are the antennae of the race, but the bullet-headed many will never learn to trust their great artists. If it is the business of the artist to make humanity aware of itself; here the thing was done, the pages of diagnosis. The multitude of wearisome fools will not learn their right hand from their left or seek out a meaning.

It is always easy for people to object to what they have not tried to understand.

I am not here to write a full volume of detailed criticism, but two things I do claim which I have not seen in reviewers' essays. First, that there was emotional greatness in Henry James's hatred of tyranny; secondly, that there was titanic volume, weight, in the masses he sets in opposition within his work. He uses forces no whit less specifically powerful than the proverbial "doom of the house,"—Destiny, *Deus ex machina,*—of great traditional art. His art was great art as opposed to over-elaborate or over-refined art by virtue of the major conflicts which he portrays. In his books he showed race against race, immutable; the essential Americanness, or Englishness or Frenchness—in *The American,* the difference between one nation and another; not flag-waving and treaties, not the machinery of government, but "why" there is always misunderstanding, why men of different race are not the same.

We have ceased to believe that we conquer anything by having Alexander the Great make a gigantic "joy-ride" through India. We know that conquests are made in the laboratory, that Curie, with his minute fragments of things seen clearly in test tubes, in curious apparati, makes conquests. So, too, in these novels, the essential qualities which make up the national qualities, are found and set working, the fundamental oppositions made clear. This is no contemptible labor. No other writer had so essayed three great nations or even thought of attempting it.

Peace comes of communication. No man of our time has so labored to create means of communication as did the late Henry James. The whole of great art is a struggle for communication. All things set against this are evil whether they be silly scoffing or obstructive tariffs.

And this communication is not a leveling, it is not an elimination of differences. It is a recognition of differences, of the right of differences to exist, of interest in finding things different. Kultur is an abomination; philology is an abomination, all repressive uniforming education is an evil.

# The Man of Letters

*by Edith Wharton*

From the first, he had an unshaken faith in his conception of the novelist's art. In 1876, when as a young and untried author he meets Flaubert, crowned with achievement, he writes: "I think I easily—more than easily—see all round him intellectually." This implied no depreciation of Flaubert's art, which he then deeply admired, but an instant perception of the narrowness of his philosophy of life. Henry James was always insisting on this point. For him every great novel must first of all be based on a profound sense of moral values ("importance of subject"), and then constructed with a classical unity and economy of means. That these two requisites should not be regarded as the measure of every work of fiction worth measuring was unintelligible; it was the inability of many of his most appreciative readers to apply the test either to his own books, or to those of others, that so bewildered and discouraged him. Subject and form—these are the fundamentals to which he perpetually reverts; and of the two (though he would hardly have admitted that they could be considered separately) subject most concerned him.

There is an inveterate tendency on the part of the Anglo-Saxon reader to regard "feeling" and "art" as antithetical. A higher sensibility is supposed by the inartistic to inhere in artless effort; and every creative writer preoccupied with the technique of his trade—from grammar and syntax to construction—is assumed to be indifferent to "subject." Even the French public, because Flaubert so overflowed to his correspondents on the importance of form and

"The Man of Letters." From *Henry James in His Letters* by Edith Wharton. The second half of her article in the *Quarterly Review* (July 1920), pp. 197-202. Reprinted by permission of the *Quarterly Review*.

the difficulties of style, seems not yet to have discovered that he also wrote: "Plus l'idée est belle, plus la phrase est sonore." Still, in France careful execution is not regarded as the direct antithesis of deep feeling. Among English-speaking readers it too commonly is: and James is still looked upon by many as a supersubtle carver of cherry stones, whereas in fact the vital matter for him was always *subject,* and the criterion of subject the extent of its moral register.

I remember his once saying, after we had seen, in Paris, a play by a brilliant young dramatist, consummate master of *la scène à faire,* but whose characters, whatever their origin or education, all wallowed in a common *muflerie:* "The trouble with eliminating the moral values is that almost all the dramatic opportunities go with them," since, where there is no revolt against the general baseness, the story, however scenic, remains on the level of what the French call a *fait divers.*

But Henry James had as keen an eye for the plastic value of "subjects" as for their moral importance. In this connection, I remember once getting an enlightening glimpse of his ideas. We were discussing Flaubert, for whom his early admiration had cooled, and for whose inner resonance I accused him of having lost his ear. James objected that Flaubert's subjects were not worth the labor spent on them; to which I returned: "But why isn't Madame Bovary as good a subject as Anna Karénine? Both novels turn upon a woman's love-affairs." "Ah," he said, "but one paints the fierce passions of a luxurious aristocracy, the other deals with the petty miseries of a little *bourgeoise* in a provincial town."

In spite of the violent foreshortening of the retort I understood what he meant, and was glad to come upon an interesting development of the idea in one of the letters to Howells, who had been pleading the boundless artistic possibilities of the local American subject, as containing "the whole of human life."

> It is on manners, customs, usages, habits, forms, upon all these things matured and established, that a novelist lives—they are the very stuff his work is made of; and in saying that in the absence of those "dreary and worn-out paraphernalia" which I enumerate as being wanting in American society, "we have simply the whole of human life left," you beg (to my sense) the question. I should say we had just so much less of it as these same "paraphernalia" represent, and I think they represent an enormous quantity of it. I shall

> feel refuted only when we have produced (setting the present high company—yourself and me—for obvious reasons apart) a gentleman who strikes me, as a novelist—as belonging to the company of Balzac and Thackeray.

It would be a mistake to think that Henry James valued the said paraphernalia for their scenic qualities, as a kind of Wardour Street setting for his situations. His meaning is best given by that penetrating phrase in *The American Scene:* "It takes a great deal of history to make a little tradition, a great deal of tradition to make a little taste, and a great deal of taste to make a little art." In other words, the successive superpositions of experience that time brings to an old and stable society seemed to him as great an asset to the novelist as to the society itself. Yet he never ceased to preach that the novelist should deal only with his own "scene," whether American or other; and there is as much sincerity as irony in the close of the same letter to Howells:

> I *must* add, however, that I applaud and esteem you highly for not feeling it; i.e. the want [of paraphernalia]. You are certainly right —magnificently and heroically right—to do so, and on the day you make your readers—I mean the readers who know and appreciate the paraphernalia—do the same, you will be the American Balzac.

Next to subject, and conterminous with it, is the great question of form. When Henry James began to write, it had not yet dawned upon English-speaking novelists that a novel might be anything other than a string of successive episodes—a "sum in addition," as he called it. It was one of his profound originalities to feel, and to illustrate in his own books, the three-dimensional qualities of that rich art which had hitherto, even in the great pages of Balzac and Thackeray, been practiced only in the flat.

For the application of the new method two things were essential: the choice of a central situation, and of what might be called centripetal incidents. To put it in another way: the tale must be treated as a stellar system, with all its episodes revolving like "the army of unalterable law" round a central *Reason Why.*

> There is, to my vision, [he writes to Mr. Wells] no authentic, and no really interesting and no *beautiful,* report of things on the novel-

ist's, the painter's part unless a particular detachment has operated. unless the great stewpot or crucible of the imagination, of the observant and recording and interpreting mind in short, has intervened and played its part.

The way of attaining this centralized vision is, as he tells Mrs. Humphry Ward, to select, among the characters of a projected novel, a reflecting consciousness, and to

"make that consciousness full, rich, universally prehensile, and *stick* to it—don't shift—and don't shift *arbitrarily*—how, otherwise, do you get your unity of subject or keep up your reader's sense of it?" To which, if you say: "How then do I get Lucy's consciousness?" I impudently retort: "By that magnificent and masterly *indirectness* which means the *only* dramatic straightness and intensity. You get it, in other words, by Eleanor." "And how does Eleanor get it?" "By *Everything*! By Lucy, by Manisty, by every pulse of the action in which she is engaged and of which she is the fullest—an exquisite—register. Go behind *her*—miles and miles; don't go behind the others, or the subject—i.e. the unity of impression—goes to smash."

And when his seemingly bewildered correspondent objects that Tolstoi and Balzac do not keep to one "consciousness," he patiently explains:

The promiscuous shiftings of standpoint and centre of Tolstoi and Balzac for instance (which come, to my eye, from their being not so much big dramatists as big *painters*—as Loti is a painter,) are the inevitable result of the *quantity of presenting* their genius launches them in. With the complexity they pile up they *can* get no clearness without trying again and again for new centres.

The rule of composition is, in short, never to be applied from the outside, but to be found in germ in each subject, as every vital principle of art must be; the one preliminary requisite being that the novelist should have the eye to find, and the hand to extract. From this stand Henry James never swerved.

What I said above, [he goes on] about the "rule" of presentation being, in each case, hard and fast, *that* I will go to the stake and burn with slow fire for—the slowest that will burn at all. I hold the artist must (infinitely!) know how he is doing it, or he is not doing it

> at all. I hold he must have a perception of the interests of his subject that grasps him as in a vise, and that (the subject being of course formulated in his mind) he sees *as* sharply the way that most presents it, and presents most of it, as against the ways that comparatively give it away. And he must there choose and stick and be consistent—and that is the hard-and-fastness and the vise. I am afraid I *do* differ with you if you mean that the picture can get any *objective* unity from any other source than that.

Again and again, to Mr. Wells in particular, he reiterates his horror of "that accurst autobiographic form which puts a premium on the loose, the improvised, the cheap, and the easy." And again, in developing the same argument to Mr. Compton Mackenzie:

> In presence of any suchlike intention I find I want a subject to be able quite definitely to state and declare itself—*as* a subject; and when the thing is communicated to me (in advance) in the form of So-and-So's doing this, that or the other, or Something-else's "happening" and so on, I kind of yearn for the expressible idea or motive, what the thing is to be done *for,* to have been presented to me; which you may say perhaps is asking a good deal. I don't think so, if any cognisance at all is vouchsafed one; it is the only thing I in the least care to ask.

The prefaces to the Definitive Edition deal exhaustively with subject and construction, but they do so with a scattered magnificence. They were the work of an ill and weary man, whose pen wanders disconcertingly from personal reminiscence to the theory of composition, and all but the most patient are left more bewildered than enlightened. I had often urged Henry James to let one of his friends—the task was meant for Mr. Lubbock—detach from those packed pages, and place in proper sequence, the chief passages on the art of fiction. The idea interested him, and should still be carried out; but meanwhile those for whom the mining of the prefaces is too arduous will find in the Letters a clearer and more accessible, if less deeply reasoned, compendium of his theory.

Henry James, as his years advanced, and his technical ability became more brilliant, fell increasingly under the spell of his formula. From being a law almost unconsciously operative it became an inexorable convention; and to turn the difficulty created by his growing reluctance to "shift the consciousness" he invented the "chorus" of unnaturally inquisitive and ubiquitous hangers-on, the Assinghams and others, who, oddly resuscitated from the classic drama (*via* Racine and Dumas *fils*) snoop and pry and report in *The Wings of the Dove, The Sacred Fount,* and *The Golden Bowl.* These pages are not concerned with the ultimate results of his art, but only with a summary of its principles as set forth in his letters; but it should at least be borne in mind that no reader who takes the theories of a great artist too literally is ever likely to surprise his secret.

One thing is certain: however much Henry James, toward the end of his life, formalized his observance and disciplined his impulses, in the service of the Genius he once so movingly invoked, he continued, to the end, to take the freest, eagerest interest in whatever was living and spontaneous in the work of his contemporaries. "I do delight in Wells; everything that he does is so alive and kicking," he once said to me; and on another occasion, speaking of Loti: "Oh, well, you see, I love Loti's books so, even when I don't like them." So his rich nature comes full circle, the intellectual and the "affective" sympathies meeting in a common glow of human kindliness and human understanding.

# The Point of View

## *The Ambassadors*

### *by Percy Lubbock*

And now for the method by which the picture of a mind is fully dramatized, the method which is to be seen consistently applied in *The Ambassadors* and the other later novels of Henry James. How is the author to withdraw, to stand aside, and to let Strether's thought tell its own story? The thing must be seen from our own point of view and no other. Author and hero, Thackeray and Esmond, Meredith and Harry Richmond, have given their various accounts of emotional and intellectual adventure; but they might do more, they might bring the facts of the adventure upon the scene and leave them to make their impression. The story passes in an invisible world, the events take place in the man's mind; and we might have to conclude that they lie beyond our reach, and that we cannot attain to them save by the help of the man himself, or of the author who knows all about him. We might have to make the best of an account at second hand, and it would not occur to us, I dare say, that anything more could be forthcoming; we seem to touch the limit of the possibilities of drama in fiction. But it is not the final limit—there is fiction here to prove it; and it is this further stroke of the art that I would now examine.

The world of silent thought is thrown open, and instead of telling the reader what happened there, the novelist uses the look and behavior of thought as the vehicle by which the story is rendered. Just as the writer of a play embodies his subject in visible action and audible speech, so the novelist, dealing with a situation like

"The Point of View." From *The Craft of Fiction* (New York: The Viking Press, Inc.; London: Jonathan Cape, Ltd., 1921) by Percy Lubbock, pp. 161-171. Reprinted by permission of the author, Jonathan Cape, Ltd., and The Viking Press, Inc.

Strether's, represents it by means of the movement that flickers over the surface of his mind. The impulses and reactions of his mood are the players upon the new scene. In drama of the theater a character must bear his part unaided; if he is required to be a desperate man, harboring thoughts of crime, he cannot look to the author to appear at the side of the stage and inform the audience of the fact; he must express it for himself through his words and deeds, his looks and tones. The playwright so arranges the matter that these will be enough, the spectator will make the right inference. But suppose that instead of a man upon the stage, concealing and betraying his thought, we watch the thought itself, the hidden thing, as it twists to and fro in his brain—watch it without any other aid to understanding but such as its own manner of bearing may supply. The novelist, more free than the playwright, could of course *tell* us, if he chose, what lurks behind this agitated spirit; he could step forward and explain the restless appearance of the man's thought. But if he prefers the dramatic way, admittedly the more effective, there is nothing to prevent him from taking it. The man's thought, in its turn, can be made to reveal its own inwardness.

Let us see how this plan is pursued in *The Ambassadors.* That book is entirely concerned with Strether's experience of his peculiar mission to Europe, and never passes outside the circle of his thought. Strether is despatched, it will be remembered, by a resolute New England widow, whose son is living lightly in Paris instead of attending to business at home. To win the hand of the widow, Strether must succeed in snatching the young man from the siren who is believed to have beguiled him. The mission is undertaken in all good faith, Strether descends upon Paris with a mind properly disposed and resolved. He comes as an ambassador representing principle and duty, to treat with the young man, appeal to him convincingly and bear him off. The task before him may be difficult, but his purpose is simple. Strether has reckoned, however, without his imagination; he had scarcely been aware of possessing one before, but everything grows complicated as it is touched and awakened on the new scene. By degrees and degrees he changes his opinion of the life of freedom; it is most unlike his prevision of it, and at last his purpose is actually inverted. He no longer sees a misguided young man to be saved from disaster, he sees an exquisite, bountiful world laid at a young man's feet; and now the only question is whether the young man is capable of meeting and grasping his opportunity. He is incapable, as it turns out; when the story ends he is on the verge of rejecting his freedom and going back to the world of commonplace; Strether's mission has ended successfully. But in Strether's mind the revolution is complete; there is nothing left for him, no reward and no future. The world of commonplace is no longer *his* world, and he is too late to seize the other; he is old, he has missed the opportunity of youth.

This is a story which must obviously be told from Strether's point of view, in the first place. The change in his purpose is due to a change in his vision, and the long slow process could not be followed unless his vision were shared by the reader. Strether's predicament, that is to say, could not be placed upon the stage; his outward behavior, his conduct, his talk, do not express a tithe of it. Only the brain behind his eyes can be aware of the color of his experience, as it passes through its innumerable gradations; and all understanding of his case depends upon seeing these. The way of the author, therefore, who takes this subject in hand, is clear enough at the outset. It is a purely pictorial subject, covering Strether's field of vision and bounded by its limits; it consists entirely of an impression received by a certain man. There can accordingly be no thought of rendering him as a figure seen from without; nothing that any one else could discern, looking at him and listening to his conversation, would give the full sense of the eventful life he is leading within. The dramatic method, as we ordinarily understand it, is ruled out at once. Neither as an action set before the reader without interpretation from within, nor yet as an action pictured for the reader by some other onlooker in the book, can this story possibly be told.

Strether's real situation, in fact, is not his open and visible situation, between the lady in New England and the young man in Paris; his grand adventure is not expressed in its incidents. These, as they are devised by the author, are secondary, they are the extension of the moral event that takes place in the breast of the ambassador, his change of mind. That is the very middle of the subject; it is a matter that lies solely between Strether himself and his vision of the free world. It is a delightful effect of irony, indeed, that he should have accomplished his errand after all, in spite of himself; but the point of the book is not there, the ironic climax only serves to bring out the point more sharply. The reversal of his own idea is underlined and enhanced by the reversal of the young man's idea in the opposite sense; but essentially the subject of the book would be unchanged if the story ended differently, if the young man held to his freedom and refused to go home. Strether would still have passed through the same cycle of unexpected experience; his errand might have failed, but still it would not have been any the more impossible for him to claim his reward, for his part, than it is impossible as things are, with the quest achieved and the young man ready to hasten back to duty of his own accord. And so the subject can only be reached through Strether's consciousness, it is plain; that way alone will command the impression that the scene makes on him. Nothing in the scene has any importance, any value in itself; what Strether sees in it—that is the whole of its meaning.

But though in *The Ambassadors* the point of view is primarily Strether's, and though it *appears* to be his throughout the book, there is in fact an insidious shifting of it, so artfully contrived that the reader may arrive at the end without suspecting the trick. The reader, all unawares, is placed in a better position for an understanding of Strether's history, better than the position of Strether himself. Using his eyes, we see what *he* sees, we are possessed of the material on which his patient thought sets to work; and that is so far well enough, and plainly necessary. All the other people in the book face toward him, and it is that aspect of them, and that only, which is shown to the reader; still more important, the beautiful picture of Paris and springtime, the stir and shimmer of life in the Rue de Rivoli and the gardens of the Tuileries, is Strether's picture, *his* vision, rendered as the time and the place strike upon his senses. All this on which his thought ruminates, the stuff that occupies it, is represented from his point of view. To see it, even for a moment, from some different angle—if, for example, the author interposed with a vision of his own—would patently disturb the right impression. The author does no such thing, it need hardly be said.

When it comes to Strether's treatment of this material, however, when it is time to learn what he makes of it, turning his experience over and over in his mind, then his own point of view no longer serves. How is anybody, even Strether, to *see* the working of his own mind? A mere account of its working, after the fact, has already been barred; we have found that this of necessity is lacking in force, it is statement where we look for demonstration. And so we must see for ourselves, the author must so arrange matters that Strether's thought will all be made intelligible by a direct view of its surface. The immediate flaw or ripple of the moment, and the next and the next, will then take up the tale, like the speakers in a dialogue which gradually unfolds the subject of the play. Below the surface, behind the outer aspect of his mind, we do not penetrate; this is drama, and in drama the spectator must judge by appearances. When Strether's mind is dramatized, nothing is shown but the passing images that anybody might detect, looking down upon a mind grown visible. There is no drawing upon extraneous sources of information; Henry James knows all there is to know of Strether, but he most carefully refrains from using his knowledge. He wishes us to accept nothing from him, on authority—only to watch and learn.

For suppose him to begin sharing the knowledge that he alone possesses, as the author and inventor of Strether; suppose that instead of representing only the momentary appearance of Strether's thought he begins to expound its substance: he must at once give us the whole of it, must let us into every secret without delay, or his exposition is plainly misleading. It is assumed that he tells all, if he once begins. And so, too, if the book were cast autobiographically and Strether spoke in person; he could not hold back, he could not heighten the story of his thought with that touch of suspense, waiting to be resolved, which stamps the impression so firmly into the memory of the onlooker. In a tale of murder and mystery there is one man who cannot possibly be the narrator, and that is the murderer himself; for if he admits us into his mind at all he must do so without reserve, thereby betraying the secret that we ought to be guessing at for ourselves. But by this method of *The Ambassadors* the mind of which the reader is made free, Strether's mind, is not given away; there is no need for it to yield up all its secrets at once. The story in it is played out by due degrees, and there may be just as much deliberation, refrainment, suspension, as in a story told scenically upon the stage. All the effect of true drama is thus at the disposal of the author, even when he seems to be describing and picturing the consciousness of one of his characters. He arrives at the point where apparently nothing but a summary and a report should be possible, and even there he is precluded from none of the privileges of a dramatist.

It is necessary to show that in his attitude toward his European errand Strether is slowly turning upon himself and looking in another direction. To announce the fact, with a tabulation of his reasons, would be the historic, retrospective, undramatic way of dealing with the matter. To bring his mind into view at the different moments, one after another, when it is brushed by new experience—to make a little scene of it, without breaking into hidden depths where the change of purpose is proceeding—to multiply these glimpses until the silent change is apparent, though no word has actually been said of it: this is Henry James's way, and though the *method* could scarcely be more devious and roundabout, always refusing the short cut, yet by these very qualities and precautions it finally produces the most direct impression, for the reader has *seen*. That is why the method is adopted. The author has so fashioned his book that his own part in the narration is now unobtrusive to the last degree; he, the author, could not imaginably figure there more discreetly. His part in the effect is no more than that of the playwright, who vanishes and leaves his people to act the story; only instead of men and women talking together, in Strether's case there are innumerable images of thought crowding across the stage, expressing the story in their behavior.

But there is more in the book, as I suggested just now, than Strether's vision and the play of his mind. In the *scenic* episodes, the colloquies that Strether holds, for example, with his sympathetic friend Maria Gostrey, another turn appears in the author's procedure. Throughout these clear-cut dialogues Strether's point of view still reigns; the only eyes in the matter are still his, there is no sight of the man himself as his companion sees him. Miss Gostrey is clearly visible, and Madame de Vionnet and little Bilham, or whoever it may be; the face of Strether himself is never turned to the reader. On the evening of the first encounter between the elderly ambassador and the young man, they sat together in a café of the boulevards and walked away at midnight through quiet streets; and all through their interview the fact of the young man's appearance is strongly dominant, for it is this that first reveals to Strether how the young man has been transformed by his commerce with the free world; and so his figure is sharply before the reader as they talk. How Strether seemed to Chad—this, too, is represented, but only by implication, through Chad's speech and manner. It is essential, of course, that it should be so, the one-sided vision is strictly enjoined by the method of the whole book. But though the seeing eye is still with Strether, there is a noticeable change in the author's way with him.

In these scenic dialogues, on the whole, we seem to have edged away from Strether's consciousness. He sees, and we with him; but when he *talks* it is almost as though we were outside him and away from him altogether. Not always, indeed; for in many of the scenes he is busily brooding and thinking throughout, and we share his mind while he joins in the talk. But still, on the whole, the author is inclined to leave Strether alone when the scene is set. He talks the matter out with Maria, he sits and talks with Madame de Vionnet, he strolls along the boulevards with Chad, he lounges on a chair in the Champs Elysées with someone else—we know the kind of scene that is set for Strether, know how very few accessories he requires, and know that the scene marks a certain definite climax, wherever it occurs, for all its everyday look. The occasion is important, there is no doubt about that; its importance is in the air. And Strether takes his part in it as though he had almost become what he cannot be, an objective figure for the reader. Evidently he cannot be that, since the center of vision is still within him; but by an easy sleight of hand the author gives him almost the value of an independent person, a man to whose words we may listen expectantly, a man whose mind is screened from us. Again and again the stroke is accomplished, and indeed there is nothing mysterious about it. Simply it consists in treating the scene as dramatically as possible—keeping it framed in Strether's vision, certainly, but keeping his consciousness out of sight, his thought unexplored. He talks to Maria; and to us, to the reader, his voice seems as much as hers to belong to somebody whom we are *watching*—which is impossible, because our point of view is his.

A small matter, perhaps, but it is interesting as a sign, still another, of the perpetual tendency of the novel to capture the advantages which it appears to forego. *The Ambassadors* is without doubt a book that deals with an entirely non-dramatic subject; it is the picture of an *état d'âme*. But just as the chapters that are concerned with Strether's soul are in the key of drama, after the fashion I have described, so too the episode, the occasion, the scene that crowns the impression, is always more dramatic in its method than it apparently has the means to be. Here, for instance, is the central scene of the whole story, the scene in the old Parisian garden, where Strether, finally filled to the brim with the sensation of all the life for which his own opportunity has passed, overflows with his passionate exhortation to little Bilham—warning him, adjuring him not to make *his* mistake, not to let life slide away ungrasped. It is the hour in which Strether touches his crisis, and the first necessity of the chapter is to show the sudden lift and heave of his mood within; the voices and admonitions of the hour, that is to say, must be heard and felt as he hears and feels them himself. The scene, then, will be given as Strether's impression, clearly, and so it is; the old garden and the evening light and the shifting company of people appear as their reflection in his thought. But the scene is *also* a piece of drama, it strikes out of the book with the strong relief of dramatic action; which is evidently an advantage gained, seeing the importance of the hour in the story, but which is an advantage that it could not enjoy, one might have said.

The quality of the scene becomes clear if we imagine the story to be told by Strether himself, narrating in the first person. Of the damage that this would entail for the picture of his brooding mind I have spoken already; but suppose the book to have taken the form of autobiography, and suppose that Strether has brought the story up to this point, where he sits beside little Bilham in Gloriani's garden. He describes the deep and agitating effect of the scene upon him, calling to him of the world he has missed; he tells what he thought and felt; and then, he says, I broke out with the following tirade to little Bilham—and we have the energetic outburst which Henry James has put into his mouth. But is it not clear how the incident would be weakened, so rendered? That speech, word for word as we have it, would lose its unexpected and dramatic quality, because Strether, arriving at it by narration, could not suddenly spring away from himself and give the impression of the worn, intelligent, clear-sighted man sitting there in the evening sun, strangely moved to unwonted eloquence. His narration must have discounted the effect of his outburst, leading us up to the very edge of it, describing how it arose, explaining where it came from. He would be *subjective,* and committed to remain so all the time.

Henry James, by his method, can secure this effect of drama, even though his Strether is apparently in the position of a narrator throughout. Strether's are the eyes, I said, and they are more so than ever during this hour in the garden; he is the sentient creature in the scene. But the author, who all through the story has been treating Strether's consciousness as a play, as an action proceeding, can at any moment use his talk almost as though the source from which it springs were unknown to us from within. I remember that he himself, in his critical preface to the book, calls attention to the way in which a conversation between Strether and Maria Gostrey, near the beginning, puts the reader in possession of all the past facts of the situation which it is necessary for him to know; a *scene* thus takes the place of that "harking back to make up," as he calls it, which is apt to appear as a lump of narrative shortly after the opening of a story. If Strether were really the narrator, whether in the first person or the third, he could not use his own talk in this manner; he would have to tell us himself about his past. But he has never *told* us his thought, we have looked at it and drawn our inferences; and so there is still some air of dramatic detachment about him, and his talk may seem on occasion to be that of a man whom we know from outside. The advantage is peculiarly felt on that crucial occasion at Gloriani's, where Strether's sudden flare of vehemence, so natural and yet so unlike him, breaks out with force unimpaired. It strikes freshly on the ear, the speech of a man whose inmost perturbations we have indeed inferred from many glimpses of his mind, but still without ever learning the full tale of them from himself.

*The Ambassadors,* then, is a story which is seen from one man's point of view, and yet a story in which that point of view is itself a matter for the reader to confront and to watch constructively. Everything in the novel is now dramatically rendered, whether it is a page of dialogue or a page of description, because even in the page of description nobody is addressing us, nobody is reporting his impression to the reader. The impression is enacting itself in the endless series of images that play over the outspread expanse of the man's mind and memory. When the story passes from these to the scenes of dialogue—from the silent drama of Strether's meditation to the spoken drama of the men and women—there is thus no break in the method. The same law rules everywhere—that Strether's changing sense of his situation shall appeal directly to the onlooker, and not by way of any summarizing picture-maker. And yet *as a whole* the book is all pictorial, an indirect impression received through Strether's intervening consciousness, beyond which the story never strays. I conclude that on this paradox the art of dramatizing the picture of somebody's experience . . . touches its limit. There is indeed no further for it to go.

# The Ghost Stories

*by Virginia Woolf*

It is plain that Henry James was a good deal attracted by the ghost story, or, to speak more accurately, by the story of the supernatural. He wrote at least eight of them, and if we wish to see what led him to do so, and what opinion he had of his success, nothing is simpler than to read his own account in the preface to the volume containing "The Altar of the Dead." Yet perhaps we shall keep our own view more distinct if we neglect the preface. As the years go by certain qualities appear, and others disappear. We shall only muddle our own estimate if we try, dutifully, to make it square with the verdict which the author at the time passed on his own work. For example, what did Henry James say of "The Great Good Place"?

> There remains "The Great Good Place" (1900)—to the spirit of which, however, it strikes me, any gloss or comment would be a tactless challenge. It embodies a calculated effect, and to plunge into it, I find, even for a beguiled glance—a course I indeed recommend—is to have left all else outside.

And to us, in 1921, "The Great Good Place" is a failure. It is another example of the fact that when a writer is completely and even ecstatically conscious of success he has, as likely as not, written his worst. We ought, we feel, to be inside, and we remain coldly outside. Something has failed to work, and we are inclined to accuse

"The Ghost Stories." (Originally entitled "Henry James's Ghost Stories.") From *Granite and Rainbow* (New York: Harcourt, Brace & World, 1921) by Virginia Woolf. 

the supernatural. The challenge may be tactless, but challenge it we must.

That "The Great Good Place" begins admirably, no one will deny. Without the waste of a word we find ourselves at once in the heart of a situation. The harassed celebrity, George Dane, is surrounded by unopened letters and unread books; telegrams arrive; invitations accumulate; and the things of value lie hopelessly buried beneath the litter. Meanwhile, Brown the manservant announces that a strange young man has arrived to breakfast. Dane touches the young man's hand, and, at this culminating point of annoyance, lapses into a trance or wakes up in another world. He finds himself in a celestial rest cure establishment. Far bells toll; flowers are fragrant; and after a time the inner life revives. But directly the change is accomplished we are aware that something is wrong with the story. The movement flags; the emotion is monotonous. The enchanter waves his wand and the cows go on grazing. All the characteristic phrases are there in waiting—the silver bowls, the melted hours—but there is no work for them to do. The story dwindles to a sweet soliloquy. Dane and the Brothers become angelic allegorical figures pacing a world that is like ours but smoother and emptier. As if he felt the need of something hard and objective the author invokes the name of the city of Bradford; but it is vain. "The Great Good Place" is an example of the sentimental use of the supernatural and for that reason no doubt Henry James would be likely to feel that he had been more than usually intimate and expressive.

The other stories will presently prove that the supernatural offers great prizes as well as great risks; but let us for a moment dwell upon the risks. The first is undoubtedly that it removes the shocks and buffetings of experience. In the breakfast room with Brown and the telegram Henry James was forced to keep moving by the pressure of reality; the door must open; the hour must strike. Directly he sank through the solid ground he gained possession of a world which he could fashion to his liking. In the dream world the door need not open; the clock need not strike; beauty is to be had for the asking. But beauty is the most perverse of spirits; it seems as if she must pass through ugliness or lie down with disorder before she can rise in her own person. The ready-made beauty of the dream world produces only an anemic and conventionalized version of the world we know. And Henry James was much too fond of the world we know to create one that we do not know. The visionary imagination was by no means his. His genius was dramatic, not lyric. Even his characters wilt in the thin atmosphere he provides for them, and we are presented with a Brother when we would much rather grasp the substantial person of Brown.

We have been piling the risks, rather unfairly, upon one story in particular. The truth is perhaps that we have become fundamentally skeptical. Mrs. Radcliffe amused our ancestors because they were our ancestors; because they lived with very few books, an occasional post, a newspaper superannuated before it reached them, in the depths of the country or in a town which resembled the more modest of our villages, with long hours to spend sitting over the fire drinking wine by the light of half a dozen candles. Nowadays we breakfast upon a richer feast of horror than served them for a twelvemonth. We are tired of violence; we suspect mystery. Surely, we might say to a writer set upon the supernatural, there are facts enough in the world to go round; surely it is safer to stay in the breakfast room with Brown. Moreover, we are impervious to fear. Your ghosts will only make us laugh, and if you try to express some tender and intimate vision of a world stripped of its hide we shall be forced (and there is nothing more uncomfortable) to look the other way. But writers, if they are worth their salt, never take advice. They always run risks. To admit that the supernatural was used for the last time by Mrs. Radcliffe and that modern nerves are immune from the wonder and terror which ghosts have always inspired would be to throw up the sponge too easily. If the old methods are obsolete, it is the business of a writer to discover new ones. The public can feel again what it has once felt—there can be no doubt about that; only from time to time the point of attack must be changed.

How consciously Henry James set himself to look for the weak place in our armor of insensibility it is not necessary to decide. Let us turn to another story, "The Friends of the Friends," and judge whether he succeeded. This is the story of a man and woman who have been trying for years to meet but only accomplish their meeting on the night of the woman's death. After her death the meetings are continued, and when this is divined by the woman he is engaged to marry she refuses to go on with the marriage. The relationship is altered. Another person, she says, has come between them. "You see her—you see her; you see her every night!" It is what we have come to call a typically Henry James situation. It is the same theme that was treated with enormous elaboration in "The Wings of the Dove." Only there, when Milly has come between Kate and Densher and altered their relationship forever she has ceased to exist; here the anonymous lady goes on with her work after death. And yet—does it make very much difference? Henry James has only to take the smallest of steps and he is over the border. His characters with their extreme fineness of perception are already half-way out of the body. There is nothing violent in their release. They seem rather to have achieved at last what they have long been attempting—communication without obstacle. But Henry James, after all, kept his ghosts for his ghost stories. Obstacles are essential to "The Wings of the Dove." When he removed them by supernatural means as he did in "The Friends of the Friends" he did so in order to produce a particular effect. The story is very short; there is no time to elaborate the relationship; but the point can be pressed home by a shock. The supernatural is brought in to provide that shock. It is the queerest of shocks—tranquil, beautiful, like the closing of chords in harmony; and yet, somehow obscene. The living and the dead by virtue of their superior sensibility have reached across the gulf; that is beautiful. The live man and the dead woman have met alone at night. They have their relationship. The spiritual and the carnal meeting together produce a strange emotion—not exactly fear, nor yet excitement. It is a feeling that we do not immediately recognize. There is a weak spot in our armor somewhere. Perhaps Henry James will penetrate by methods such as these.

Next, however, we turn to "Owen Wingrave," and the enticing game of pinning your author to the board by detecting once more traces of his fineness, his subtlety, whatever his prevailing characteristics may be, is rudely interrupted. Pinioned, tied down, to all appearance lifeless, up he jumps and walks away. Somehow one has forgotten to account for the genius, for the driving power which is so incalculable and, so essential. With Henry James in particular we tend, in wonder at his prodigious dexterity, to forget that he had a crude and simple passion for telling stories. The preface to Owen Wingrave throws light upon that fact, and incidentally suggests why it is that Owen Wingrave as a ghost story misses its mark. One summer's afternoon, many years ago, he tells us, he sat on a penny chair under a great tree in Kensington Gardens. A slim young man sat down upon another chair near by and began to read a book.

> Did the young man then, on the spot, just *become* Owen Wingrave, establishing by the mere magic of type the situation, creating at a stroke all the implications and filling out all the picture? . . . my poor point is only that at the beginning of my session in the penny chair the seedless fable hadn't a claim to make or an excuse to give, and that, the very next thing, the pennyworth still partly unconsumed, it was fairly bristling with pretexts. "Dramatise it, dramatise it!" would seem to have rung with sudden intensity in my ears.

So the theory of a conscious artist taking out his little grain of matter and working it into the finished fabric is another of our critical fables. The truth appears to be that he sat on a chair, saw a young man, and fell asleep. At any rate, once the group, the man, or perhaps only the sky and the trees become significant, the rest is there inevitably. Given Owen Wingrave, then Spencer Coyle, Mrs. Coyle, Kate Julian, the old house, the season, the atmosphere must be in existence. Owen Wingrave implies all that. The artist has simply to see that the relations between these places and people are the right ones. When we say that Henry James had a passion for storytelling we mean that when his significant moment came to him the accessories were ready to flock in.

In this instance they flocked in almost too readily. There they are on the spot with all the stir and importance that belong to living people. Miss Wingrave seated in her Baker-street lodging with "a fat catalogue of the Army and Navy Stores, which reposed on a vast desolate table-cover of false blue"; Mrs. Coyle, "a fair fresh slow woman," who admitted and indeed gloried in the fact that she was in love with her husband's pupils, "which shows that the subject between them was treated in a liberal spirit"; Spencer Coyle himself, and the boy Lechmere—all bear of course upon the question of Owen's temperament and situation, and yet they bear on so many other things besides. We seem to be settling in for a long absorbing narrative; and then, rudely, incongruously, a shriek rings out; poor Owen is found stretched on the threshold of the haunted room; the supernatural has cut the book in two. It is violent; it is sensational; but if Henry James himself were to ask us, "Now, have I frightened you?" we should be forced to reply, "Not a bit." The catastrophe has not the right relations to what has gone before. The vision in Kensington Gardens did not, perhaps, embrace the whole. Out of sheer bounty the author has given us a scene rich in possibilities—a young man whose problem (he detests war and is condemned to be a soldier) has a deep psychological interest; a girl whose subtlety and oddity are purposely defined as if in readiness for future use. Yet what use is made of them? Kate Julian has merely to dare a young man to sleep in a haunted room; a plump Miss from a parsonage would have done as well. What use is made of the supernatural? Poor Owen Wingrave is knocked on the head by the ghost of an ancestor; a stable bucket in a dark passage would have done it better.

The stories in which Henry James uses the supernatural effectively are, then, those where some quality in a character or in a situation can only be given its fullest meaning by being cut free from facts. Its progress in the unseen world must be closely related to what goes on in this. We must be made to feel that the apparition fits the crisis of passion or of conscience which sent it forth so exactly that the ghost story, besides its virtues as a ghost story, has the additional charm of being also symbolical. Thus the ghost of Sir Edmund Orme appears to the lady who jilted him long ago whenever her daughter shows signs of becoming engaged. The apparition is the result of her guilty conscience, but it is more than that. It is the guardian of the rights of lovers. It fits what has gone before; it completes. The use of the supernatural draws out a harmony which would otherwise be inaudible. We hear the first note close at hand, and then, a moment after, the second chimes far away.

Henry James's ghosts have nothing in common with the violent old ghosts—the blood-stained sea captains, the white horses, the headless ladies of dark lanes and windy commons. They have their origin within us. They are present whenever the significant overflows our powers of expressing it; whenever the ordinary appears ringed by the strange. The baffling things that are left over, the frightening ones that persist—these are the emotions that he takes, embodies, makes consoling and companionable. But how can we be afraid? As the gentleman says when he has seen the ghost of Sir Edmund Orme for the first time: "I am ready to answer for it to all and sundry that ghosts are much less alarming and much more amusing than was commonly supposed." The beautiful urbane spirits are only not of this world because they are too fine for it. They have taken with them across the border their clothes, their manners, their breeding, their band-boxes, and valets and ladies' maids. They remain always a little worldly. We may feel clumsy in their presence, but we cannot feel afraid. What does it matter, then, if we do pick up "The Turn of the Screw" an hour or so before bedtime? After an exquisite entertainment we shall, if the other stories are to be trusted, end with this fine music in our ears, and sleep the sounder.

Perhaps it is the silence that first impresses us. Everything at Bly is so profoundly quiet. The twitter of birds at dawn, the far-away cries of children, faint footsteps in the distance stir it but leave it unbroken. It accumulates; it weighs us down; it makes us strangely apprehensive of noise. At last the house and garden die out beneath it. "I can hear again, as I write, the intense hush in which the sounds of evening dropped. The rooks stopped cawing in the golden sky, and the friendly hour lost for the unspeakable minute all its voice." It is unspeakable. We know that the man who stands on the tower staring down at the governess beneath is evil. Some unutterable obscenity has come to the surface. It tries to get in; it tries to get at something. The exquisite little beings who lie innocently asleep must at all costs be protected. But the horror grows. Is it possible that the little girl, as she turns back from the window, has seen the woman outside? Has she been with Miss Jessel? Has Quint visited the boy? It is Quint who hangs about us in the dark; who is there in that corner and again there in that. It is Quint who must be reasoned away, and for all our reasoning returns. Can it be that we are afraid? But it is not a man with red hair and a white face whom we fear. We are afraid of something unnamed, of something, perhaps, in ourselves. In short, we turn on the light. If by its beams we examine the story in safety, note how masterly the telling is, how each sentence is stretched, each image filled, how the inner world gains from the robustness of the outer, how beauty and obscenity twined together worm their way to the depths—still we must own that something remains unaccounted for. We must admit that Henry James has conquered. That courtly, worldly, sentimental old gentleman can still make us afraid of the dark.

# A Prediction

*by T. S. Eliot*

Henry James is an author who is difficult for English readers, because he is an American; and who is difficult for Americans, because he is a European; and I do not know whether he is possible to other readers at all. On the other hand, the exceptionally sensitive reader, who is neither English nor American, may have a position of detachment which is an advantage. One thing is certain, that the books of Henry James form a complete whole. One must read all of them, for one must grasp, if anything, both the unity and the progression. The gradual development, and the fundamental identity of spirit, are both important, and their lesson is one lesson.

James has suffered the usual fate of those who, in England, have outspokenly insisted on the importance of technique. His technique has received the kind of praise usually accorded to some useless, ugly, and ingenious piece of carving which has taken a very long time to make; and he is widely reproached for not succeeding in doing the things that he did not attempt to do. With "character," in the sense in which the portrayal of character is usually expected in the English novel, he had no concern; but his critics do not understand that "character" is only one of the ways in which it is possible to grasp at reality: had James been a better hand at character, he would have been a coarser hand altogether, and would have missed the sensibility to the peculiar class of data which were his province. And the fact that, an American, his view of England—a view which very gradually dissolves in his development—was a

"A Prediction." From *A Prediction in Regard to Three English Authors* by T. S. Eliot, *Vanity Fair* (February 1924). Reprinted by permission of the author.

romantic view, is a small matter. His romanticism implied no defect in observation of the things that he wanted to observe; it was not the romanticism of those who dream because they are too lazy or too fearful to face the fact; it issues, rather, from the imperative insistence of an ideal which tormented him. He was possessed by the vision of an ideal society; he *saw* (not fancied) the relations between the members of such a society. And no one, in the end, has ever been more aware—or with more benignity, or less bitterness—of the disparity between possibility and fact. If his completed work failed to prove that, his last unfinished novels (*The Sense of the Past* and *The Ivory Tower*) could hardly fail to do so.

The example which Henry James offered us was not that of a style to imitate, but of an integrity so great, a vision so exacting, that it was forced to the extreme of care and punctiliousness for exact expression. James did not provide us with "ideas," but with another world of thought and feeling. For such a world some have gone to Dostoievsky, some to James; and I am inclined to think that the spirit of James, so much less violent, with so much more reasonableness and so much more resignation than that of the Russian, is no less profound, and is more useful, more applicable, for our future.

# The Pilgrimage

## I
*by Van Wyck Brooks*

The main alternative had always been flight, and this fact had given birth to "the classic debate of American culture. Should an American artist stay at home?" (I am quoting Waldo Frank's *In the American Jungle*). This I had set out to study in the case of Henry James, the greatest of all the American expatriates or exiles. It seemed to me obvious that "something went wrong with his development," as one of his English admirers, F. R. Leavis, was to observe in time in *The Great Tradition.* Following somewhat the same line that I had taken years before, this critic rejected as "bad" or "not successful" the three long later novels of Henry James, *The Ambassadors, The Golden Bowl* and *The Wings of the Dove,* adding that the famous Prefaces were "not merely difficult but unrewarding," while he took one back to this writer's "happiest" phase. He described *The Bostonians* and *The Portrait of a Lady* as "the two most brilliant novels in the language," saying that, with them and with *Washington Square* and other novels of their time, James's genius functioned at its "freest and fullest." Then what Dr. Leavis called the "hypertrophy of technique" set in and we had the indirections and subtleties of James's decline.

This was precisely what I had said in *The Pilgrimage of Henry James,* although, as it happened, Dr. Leavis, agreeing with my verdict, disagreed with my explanation of it. Yet it seemed to me equally obvious that James, as his brother William said, had lost touch with the "vital facts of human character," and this was because he had lost touch with the people whom he understood, his fellow-Americans either at home or in Europe. In short, he had "forfeited" the "precious advantage in ceasing to tread his native soil" that James imputed to Hawthorne just at the moment when he also said of Turgenev, regarding this matter of the "native soil," that "all great novelists savor strongly of it." He had also said it was dangerous for a novelist "to project himself into an atmosphere in which he has not a transmitted and inherited property"; and was it not evident that he himself failed to assimilate as a novelist should the English world that he had set out to conquer? Why, otherwise, after a few attempts to write as an English novelist, did he revert to the abandoned American themes, to the "international subject" that had long since "faded" from his mind, as he had said so emphatically years before?

Of course, all this was to mean little to the critics of a later time for whom indirectness and "difficulty" were positive values, who cared nothing for "character," the "air of reality" or the "solidity of specification" that James himself had called the "supreme virtues" of fiction. They loved his "crooked corridors" in the face of Tolstoy, who wished to get "at once down to business" when he began the greatest of the world's novels, and they were not dissatisfied with James's ghostlike presences floating in a void, shadowlike passionless women and fish-blooded men. It meant little to them that his later fictions were like cobwebs, as Somerset Maugham remarked, "which at any moment the housemaid's broom with brutal common sense may sweep away," for the formalist critics, unconcerned with literature in its relation to life, cared for problems of texture and structure only. But as, more and more, with the passing of time, they dominated the critical world, I questioned, as Whitman had done, these "professional elects," feeling that people of ripe heart and mind who know the world as they know life are always the ultimate judges of the value of novels. (In that sense, Desmond MacCarthy was undoubtedly right when he said, "The public is the critic.") As I knew these people, they usually agreed with William James, who wrote to his brother that "the *core* of literature is solid," and who remarked to another correspondent, "I for one am no longer able to read a word that he [Henry] writes." Yet who was more interested than William James in every phase of real life and in every novel that gave one a feeling for it? He was not a Philistine, as the lovers of Henry James implied when they were obliged to face this condemnation.

So I might have felt sure that I was right in the general estimate of James's work that Dr. Leavis confirmed a few years later, and it struck me as an interesting fact that five novelists wrote to me to say that they agreed with my conclusions. They were all writers of integrity of the older generation who had attempted themselves to novelize the country and who might have been supposed to wish that Henry James had failed when he himself gave up the attempt to do so. But I do not think this was the motive that turned them against his later work, as John Jay Chapman rejected James altogether, saying, "I am so out of sympathy with his temperament that I have never read him, but I read your book . . . muttering all the time that the vaporous subject was not worth" the treatment, "yet feeling it was all true." What Chapman called James's vaporousness was the general objection, and to Ellen Glasgow, who had met him in London several times, James, so unlike Hardy, "seemed to ring hollow." It shocked Robert Herrick, for the rest, that James denatured his early work when he rewrote the conversations in it, when his Christopher Newmans and Longmores ceased to be their American selves and generally spoke in the later Jamesian manner. Aside from this, Herrick was repelled by the "pathetic provincialism" of Henry James's relation to the world he had adopted. He had corrected this young man for addressing him as "Mr. James," saying, "Only butlers do that, my dear Herrick."

With so much corroboration, my mind should have been at rest, I should have felt that for me the case was settled, especially when so many others felt as I did, when, for one, AE, challenging James's false air of profundity, said that he "made intricacies in the shallows." Then there was Paul Elmer More, who, praising Anthony Trollope, spoke of the "endless chatter" of the later Henry James, together with his "tangled sleave of oblique suggestions," —all of which justified my regret that James had been taken as a model by many beginning novelists in this country. For was he not inevitably sterilizing as an influence on others? He warned them away from more congruous models like Tolstoy or Dostoievsky, whom he called "baggy monsters" or "mere fluid puddings," and, imposing upon them his own "right" form, he kept them from finding their own form, which ought to have sprung out of their subject matter. Moreover, he induced in them a kind of literary opiumism in which the realities of character ceased to matter and life and love were felt to be somehow vulgar.

So I was convinced most of the time, but—to continue with my doubts—was this all really due to expatriation, evident as it so often was that the American émigré seemed to lose in Europe his natural bearings? There was Edith Wharton whose work deteriorated more and more after she had "cut her roots," in the phrase of Percy Lubbock, as if to prove that the American mind could not maintain its integrity abroad, that it was all but inevitably compromised in Europe. Why else did Henry James himself say so often to American friends that he should not have lost touch with his countrypeople, and was it not the moral of his life of Story that American artists might better stay at home? Both James and Edith Wharton were perpetually troubled by a sense that their literary lives might have been built on a mistake, that perhaps Dostoievsky was right for them when he said, "A writer should not leave his country for too long a time. He should live one life with her. Otherwise he is lost." But I had set out to make a case and I could not be sure of it, for there were other possible explanations of James's anomalous development or failure to develop, and I was "harried with doubts," as Arnold Bennett said he was when he too attacked James's later novels. For him *The Golden Bowl* was an "arid desert." Was I insensitive, was I blind to an obvious greatness? I felt that for nothing in the world would I ever open again any of Henry James's later novels and that his appearance of depth was wholly an illusion; and yet regarding all this I fell into a state of irresolution that actually became for me a virulent illness. Along with one or two other circumstances, it carried me into a formidable nervous breakdown.

Nor was I encouraged later to feel that I was right when James became one of the idols of a long generation, when the new critics defended his last phase as the major phase and no university was complete without a "Henry James expert." The new climate of opinion in literature, largely created in Paris, had been created wholly by expatriated persons, Pound, Eliot, Gertrude Stein, Joyce,

Ford and Lawrence, exiles from their respective countries who could not feel that literature had any vital connection with "native lands." The writer for them was above localities and countries, and, moreover, they were not greatly interested in character as such or the "old-fashioned human element," as D. H. Lawrence called it. People were apt to seem to them as they seemed to Wyndham Lewis, "rather walking notions than 'real' entities," and so there was nothing amiss for them in the later Henry James with his "No. 1" and "No. 2" young men. Meanwhile, when questions of technique filled the minds of critics, he had much of technical interest for them, at a time, moreover, when the religion of art had become virtually the only religion. With the "divine principle" of his work, the "sacred years" that he had known and his "celestial, soothing, sanctifying process," James surrounded himself with an aura of priesthood.

For the rest, with the new generation, the old question of colonialism had gone by the board, and so had the other old question of expatriation. They had ceased to have any meaning for the younger writers, while I myself had been involved in both; and I was to realize, looking back, that I had been quarreling with myself when I appeared to be quarreling with Henry James. For, like many of my friends, I too had been enchanted with Europe, and I had vaguely hoped to continue to live there. It struck me that if I was always "straining to read the face of America"—Paul Rosenfeld's phrase for my obsession—it was because of an over-determination, and perhaps the question of expatriation had so possessed my mind because this mind itself had been divided. Only my reason had told me what I later came to feel, that the French aphorist Doudon was right when he said, "One must live, struggle and die among one's own." I mean he was right for those who were organized as I was.

In the end the question of Henry James resolved itself for me in a certain general notion of literary values—that there is a gulf in judgment and feeling between those who see literature in terms of itself and those who see it in terms of a wider connection. In this respect and regarding James, I stood in the second category with AE, Maugham, More, Bennett and an army of others, minds as diverse as they well could be yet all agreeing that substance and depth are indispensable elements of a great novel. They might have agreed that James was a fine literary artist without ceasing to feel that his later work was poor indeed in qualities that are still more important than literary art. Was it not irrelevant to ask, as James asked of Tolstoy and Dostoievsky, "What do they artistically mean?"—for, baggy monsters that they were, along with Dickens, in James's mind, they were no less than supreme as both novelists and writers. And as so many novelists of our own 'twenties lost their substance and grasp of life, it struck me that the case of James was really a symbol—I mean those novelists who had grown up in the so-called expatriate religion of art with a feeling that native lands are not important. Judging by these later cases, it seemed to me disastrous for the novelist to lose his natural connection with an inherited world that is deeply his own, when, ceasing to be "in the pedigree" of his own country, he is no longer an expression of the communal life.

# The Pilgrimage

## II
*by Edmund Wilson*

It is becoming a commonplace to say of Mr. Van Wyck Brooks that he is really a social historian rather than a literary critic, but one cannot avoid raising the question in connection with his new book. *The Pilgrimage of Henry James,* like *The Ordeal of Mark Twain,* is a page of American social history: in it, Henry James figures as the type of sensitive and imaginative American who, in the later nineteenth century, found the United States too barren and too crude for him and sought a more congenial environment in Europe. Mr. Brooks points out James's original isolation as the son of the elder Henry James, that well-to-do wandering philosopher who traveled back and forth between Boston and New York, between the United States and Europe, without finding himself quite at home anywhere; and he traces James's first saturation with European impressions during the formative years of his teens; his attempt at the beginning of his career to establish himself in America as an American novelist working with native material; his discouragement, his longing for Europe, his experiments with France and Italy and his dissatisfaction with his life there; his decision to live permanently in England and to find a field for his art in the depiction of English society; his failure, after years of living among them, to establish intimate relations with the English and his disillusioned reaction against them; the bankruptcy of his imagination, his homesickness and his visit to the United States; his consternation and despair at the spectacle of modern America, and his final return to England. In short, Henry James's tragedy,

"The Pilgrimage." (Originally entitled "The Pilgrimage of Henry James.") From *The Shores of Light* (New York: Farrar, Straus & Young, Inc., 1952) by Edmund Wilson, pp. 217-228. 

according to Mr. Brooks, was that of the literary artist who has lost contact with his own society without having been able to strike roots in any other. And of all this aspect of James's career he has given the most intelligent and the most exhaustive account that we have yet had; in fact, it may be said that James's social significance and the part that his social situation plays in his work have here been properly appreciated for the first time. Mr. Brooks has made a contribution of permanent value toward the criticism of Henry James. He has interpreted the complex subject with all his incomparable instinct for divining the feelings and motives of Americans, for getting under their skins; and he has presented his logical theory with the consummate orderliness, neatness and point that he always brings to making out a case. When, for example, he disentangles James's reasons for turning playwright at one period of his career, he generates a kind of excitement in the process of demonstration that seems almost to be independent of the interest of what is being demonstrated. And he has reduced the whole to an entertaining narrative colored by imagination and written with grace. From the point of view of literary form, Mr. Brooks's *Henry James* is, in fact, probably the best of his books.

Where the book is unsatisfactory is in its failure to recognize the real nature and development of James's art. Mr. Brooks has completely subordinated Henry James the artist to Henry James the social symbol, with the result that James's literary work, instead of being considered in its integrity on its own merits, has undergone a process of lopping and distortion to make it fit the Procrustes bed of a thesis. According to Mr. Brooks's simplification, Henry James was at first a very good novelist and then, later on, a very bad one. Mr. Brooks admires James's earlier fiction as a Turgenev-like social document and writes a warm appreciation of it—that is, he admires James in direct proportion as James performs the same sort of function as Mr. Brooks himself. But what he says, in effect, is that, after the publication of *The Bostonians* in 1886, James's artistic record is an almost total blank: when James had settled in England and had used up his American impressions, his failure to make anything of his English material was virtually complete. Mr. Brooks here lumps together the work of thirty years and, in the interest of an a priori theory, refuses to admit distinctions among some thirty volumes of fiction of widely differing character and merit. The truth is that the work of James's English residence falls into three distinct periods. During the second of these—after *The Bostonians* and while he is already dealing chiefly with English material—he reaches what seems to me indisputably his completest artistic maturity: he has got over a certain stiffness, a certain naïveté, which characterized his earlier work and he has acquired a new flexibility and a personal idiom. He has come for the first time into the full possession of his language and form, and he has not yet lost any of the vividness of his youthful imagination. He has ten years ahead of him still before that imagination will begin to show signs of flagging in such books as *The Awkward Age,* and longer still before that style runs to seed in the thickets of the later novels. In the meantime, in the fiction of this period—particularly, perhaps, in the shorter novels which were characteristic of it: *What Maisie Knew,* "The Aspern Papers," etc.—he is to produce what seems to the present writer his most satisfactory and distinguished work. As for the deterioration which afterwards sets in, it is to be ascribed chiefly to advancing age. An important thing to remember in connection with James's latest novels—which Mr. Brooks treats with such severity—is that *The Ambassadors, The Wings of the Dove* and *The Golden Bowl* were all written when James was in his late fifties. Their abstraction, their comparative dimness and their exaggerated mannerisms are such as not infrequently appear in the work of an artist's later years. George Meredith and Robert Browning, who did not labor under the handicap of being expatriated Americans, developed somewhat similar traits. These later novels of James are, in any case, not as Mr. Brooks asserts, fundamentally unreal and weak. Intellectually, they are perhaps the most vigorous, the most heroically conceived, of his fictions; but they are like tapestries from which, though the design and the figures still remain masterfully outlined, the colors are fading out.

When all this has been said, however, there still confronts us, in connection with James, the question of a lack in his work of direct emotional experience—a lack which is naturally felt more disconcertingly in his later than in his earlier books, since it is less easily comprehensible in a mature than in a callow man. One can agree here with Mr. Brooks that this insufficient experience of personal relations may be partly accounted for by James's isolation among the English. Yet to throw all the emphasis thus on James's social situation, as Mr. Brooks seems to do, is surely to proceed from the wrong direction. James's solitude, his emotional starvation, his inhibitions against entering into life, were evidently the result of his fundamental moral character, not merely an accident of his social maladjustment; and with the problem of that fundamental character Mr. Brooks never adequately deals. "An immortal symbol," he sums James up, "the embodiment of that impossible yearning of which Hawthorne somewhere speaks—the yearning of the American in the Old World" for the past from which he has been separated. But this theory that a man's whole career may hinge on his yearning for the European past is humanly unconvincing.

It is precisely because Mr. Brooks's interest is all social and never moral that he has missed the point of James's art. It is possible for him to find James's work so empty and disappointing only because he insists on comparing it with that of writers with whom James has little in common: Hardy, Dickens, Tolstoy and Balzac. One would be in a position to appreciate James better if one compared him with the dramatists of the seventeenth century—Racine and Molière, whom he resembles in form as well as in point of view, and even Shakespeare, when allowance has been made for the most extreme differences in subject and form. These poets are not, like Dickens and Hardy, writers of melodrama—either humorous or pessimistic, nor secretaries of society like Balzac, nor prophets like Tolstoy: they are occupied simply with the presentation of conflicts of moral character, which they do not concern themselves about softening or averting. They do not indict society for these situations: they regard them as universal and inevitable. They do not even blame God for allowing them: they accept them as the conditions of life. Titus and Bérénice, Alceste and Célimène, Antony and Octavius—these are forces which, once set in motion, are doomed to irreconcilable opposition. The dramatist makes no attempt to decide between competing interests: he is content to understand his characters and to put their behavior before us.

Now, it was James's immense distinction to have brought to

contemporary life something of this "classical" point of view. The conflicts in his early novels are likely to be presented in terms of European manners and morals at odds with American ones—with a predisposition in favor of the latter. But later on, James's contrasts tend to take on a different aspect: they represent, not merely national divergences, but antagonisms of ideals and temperaments of a kind that may occur anywhere. I cannot agree with Mr. Brooks when he says that in James's later novels "the 'low sneaks' have it all their own way . . . the subtle are always the prey of the gross . . . the pure in heart are always at the mercy of those that work iniquity." On the contrary, the leaning toward melodrama that allowed James in his earlier novels to play virtuous Americans off against scoundrelly Europeans has almost entirely disappeared. *The Ambassadors* is obviously a sort of attempt to re-do the theme of *The American,* as *The Wings of the Dove* is to re-do that of *The Portrait of a Lady*; but one has only to compare the two pairs of books to realize that James no longer sees life in terms of the innocent and the guilty. The Bellegarde family in the earlier novel are cold-blooded and impenitent villains, whereas Mme. de Vionnet, who plays a somewhat similar role in *The Ambassadors,* is shown in as attractive a light as the American to whom she is morally opposed; in the same way Gilbert Osmond and his mistress, who make Isabel Archer miserable, are a good deal more theatrical than Kate Croy and her lover, who try to exploit Milly Theale. Mr. Brooks's account of *The Wings of the Dove* seems almost perversely unintelligent. He melodramatically describes Milly Theale as the "victim of the basest plot that ever a mind conceived"; yet one of the most remarkable things about *The Wings of the Dove* is the way in which, from the very first pages, Henry James succeeds in making us sympathize with the author of this unquestionably ignoble plot, in making us feel that what she does is inevitable. Kate Croy, though hard and crass, is striving for the highest aspirations she is capable of understanding, just as the more fastidious Milly is.

It is thus, in James's later novels, not a case of the pure in heart invariably falling a prey to the guilty, of the low sneaks having it their own way. It is simply a struggle between different kinds of people with different kinds of needs. I do not know what Mr.

Brooks means when he writes of "the constant abrogation of James's moral judgment, in these years of an enchanted exile in a museum world" nor when he says that James "had seen life, in his own way, as all the great novelists have seen it, *sub specie aeternitatis;* he was to see it henceforth, increasingly, *sub specie mundi.*" On the contrary, James, in his later works, is just as much concerned with moral problems, and he is able to see all around them as he has not been able to do before. He has come to be occupied here even more than in his earlier work with what seem to him the irremediable antagonisms of interest between people who enjoy themselves without inhibitions, who take all they can get from life, and people who are curbed by scruples of aesthetic taste as well as of morality from following all their impulses and satisfying all their appetites—between the worldly, the selfish, the "splendid," and the dutiful, the sensitive, the humble. This humility, this moral rectitude takes on in Henry James the aspect of a moral beauty which he opposes, as it were, to the worldly kind; both kinds of beauty attract him, he understands the points of view of the devotees of both, but it is one of his deepest convictions that you cannot have both at the same time. The point of *What Maisie Knew,* for example, lies in the contrast between Maisie's other guardians—the vivid, the charming or the bold—who live only for their own pleasure and advantage and refuse to be bothered with her, and Mrs. Wix, the ridiculous old governess, who, by reason of her possession of a "moral sense," is left with the responsibility of Maisie, "to work her fingers to the bone." So, in *The Golden Bowl,* the brilliant figures of Charlotte and the Prince are contrasted with the unselfishness and the comparative dreariness of Maggie Verver and her father. Almost all Henry James's later novels, in one way or another, illustrate this theme. Surely this, and not, as Mr. Brooks suggests, any mere technical pattern, is that "figure in the carpet" that is hinted at in the famous short story; and in this tendency to oppose the idea of a good conscience to the idea of doing what one likes—wearing, as it does so often in James, the aspect of American versus European—there is evidently a Puritan survival that Mr. Brooks, in his capacity as specialist in American habits of thought, might have been expected to treat more prominently. As it is, he only touches upon it by way of a different route.

Of Mr. Brooks's queer use of his documents for the purpose of proving the artistic nullity of the latter half of James's career, many instances might be given. We sometimes get a little the impression that, instead of reading James's novels with a sense of them as artistic wholes, he has been combing them intently for passages that would seem to bear out his thesis even in cases where, taken in context, they clearly have a different meaning. The extreme abuse of this method is to be found in the chapter in which Mr. Brooks attempts to prove the inadmissible assertion that none of James's later novels is "the fruit of an artistic impulse that is at once spontaneous and sustained," that they "are all—given in each case the tenuity of the idea—stories of the 'eight to ten thousand words' blown out to the dimensions of novels." One would ask oneself at once: In what way can the "ideas" of *The Ambassadors* and *The Wings of the Dove* be described as being any more "tenuous" than those of their predecessors? How could either of them conceivably be a short story? They cover as long a period as the early novels, they contain just as many important characters, they deal with themes of just the same nature and they are worked out on just as elaborate a scale. But Mr. Brooks does not even pretend to go to the novels themselves in order to justify his critical conclusions about them: he bases his whole case on three passages which he has found in James's correspondence. When we come to examine these, we discover that two of them are references, respectively, to the "long-windedness" of *The Wings of the Dove* and the "vague verbosity" of *The Golden Bowl*—which certainly does not prove in the least that the author thought their *ideas* tenuous. It is in the third of these references that the phrase about "the tenuity of the idea" occurs, in an entirely different connection. James writes apologetically to Howells in regard to *The Sacred Fount* that it had been "planned, like *The Spoils of Poynton, What Maisie Knew,* 'The Turn of the Screw' and various others, as a story of the 'eight to ten thousand words' " and had then spun itself out much longer. He goes on to explain that he might, perhaps, have "chucked" *The Sacred Fount* in the middle if he had not had a superstition about not finishing things. He does not, however, say that he considers these other novels as unsatisfactory as *The Sacred Fount* nor that he had any impulse to chuck them. In the only part of this passage, moreover, that Mr. Brooks omits to quote, he gives a quite different explanation from Mr. Brooks's one for his practice, at this particular time, of projecting short stories instead of novels: *"The Sacred Fount,"* writes James, "is one of several things of mine, in these last years, that have paid the penalty of having been conceived only as the 'short story' that (alone apparently) I could hope to work off somewhere (which I mainly failed of)." That is, he planned short stories rather than novels, because he thought that short stories were more salable. That, against this intention, he should have found the short stories growing uncontrollably into novels would seem to prove, not, as Mr. Brooks says, that James's "artistic impulse" was not "spontaneous and sustained," but, on the contrary, precisely that it was.

Mr. Brooks's misrepresentation of the obvious sense of this passage, his readiness to found upon such meager evidence so sweeping and damning a case, throws rather an unreassuring light on the spirit of his recent criticism. That spirit is one of intense zeal at the service of intense resentment. What Mr. Brooks resents and desires to protest against is the spiritual proverty of America and our discouragement of the creative artist. But, in preaching this doctrine, Mr. Brooks has finally allowed his bitterness to far overshoot its mark and to castigate the victims of American conditions along with the conditions themselves. In the latter part of *The Pilgrimage of Henry James,* we have the feeling that he has set out to show James up, just as, in his earlier one, he set out to show up Mark Twain. The story of Henry James, like that of Mark Twain, might have excited both our pity and our admiration; but in Mr. Brooks's hands, it gives rise to little but irony. Like Mr. Sinclair Lewis, that other exposer of the spiritual poverty of America, Mr. Brooks has little charity for the poor, and his enthusiasm for creative genius is not today sufficiently generous to prevent him, one is coming to feel, from deriving a certain satisfaction from describing its despair and decay.

There are, however, in any case, two reasons why Henry James is not a very happy subject for Mr. Van Wyck Brooks. In the first place, for all the sobriety of Mr. Brooks's tone, he is in reality a romantic and a preacher, who has little actual sympathy or comprehension for the impersonal and equanimous writer like James.

One remembers in this connection a curious passage about Shakespeare in *America's Coming of Age*: "Why is it," asked Mr. Brooks, "that Shakespeare is never the master of originating minds? Plato may be, or Dante, or Tolstoy . . . but not Shakespeare . . . certainly anyone who requires a lesson of Shakespeare comes away with nothing but grace and good humor." The truth is that Mr. Brooks cannot help expecting a really great writer to be a stimulating social prophet. He can understand the lessons conveyed by a Plato or a Tolstoy, but he seems not much more responsive to Shakespeare than he is to Henry James. From Shakespeare he comes away with "nothing but grace and good humor," and from James with almost nothing at all. In the second place, Henry James lends himself to Mr. Brooks's treatment a good deal less satisfactorily than, say, Mark Twain, because the latter was admittedly a remarkable figure who wrote a few very fine things but the bulk of whose books, partly hack-work, have very little literary interest. In this case, it may be said that the man is more impressive than his work, and Mr. Brooks is in a position to tell us something important about him which is not to be found in his writings. But, in the case of Henry James, the work he accomplished in his lifetime is infinitely more interesting than the man. Henry James was not an intimidated and sidetracked artist, but a writer who understood both himself and the society in which he was living and who was able to say just what he meant about nations and human beings. It is difficult for Mr. Brooks to tell us anything about Henry James that James has not told us himself. *The Pilgrimage of Henry James,* which is shorter than its predecessor, falls short of it, also, in life and force. The *Mark Twain* was driven along by the author's passion of discovery and his fury of indignation to a conclusion which is, I suppose, so far Mr. Brooks's highest point of eloquence; but it is perhaps, in the later book, a sign of the critic's failure to be fully possessed by his subject, of his comparatively feeble reaction to it, that the last page, instead of leaving us, as its predecessor did, with a dramatic and significant image, should be evidently an unconscious imitation of the last page of Lytton Strachey's *Queen Victoria.*

# *The Ambassadors*

## *by E. M. Forster*

Let us examine at some length another book of the rigid type, a book with a unity, and in this sense an easy book, although it is by Henry James. We shall see in it pattern triumphant, and we shall also be able to see the sacrifices an author must make if he wants his pattern and nothing else to triumph.

*The Ambassadors,* like *Thaïs,* is the shape of an hourglass. Strether and Chad, like Paphnuce and Thaïs, change places, and it is the realization of this that makes the book so satisfying at the close. The plot is elaborate and subtle, and proceeds by action or conversation or mediation through every paragraph. Everything is planned, everything fits; none of the minor characters are just decorative like the talkative Alexandrians at Nicias' banquet; they elaborate on the main theme, they work. The final effect is prearranged, dawns gradually on the reader, and is completely successful when it comes. Details of the intrigue may be forgotten, but the symmetry created is enduring.

Let us trace the growth of this symmetry.[1]

Strether, a sensitive middle-aged American, is commissioned by his old friend, Mrs. Newsome, whom he hopes to marry, to go to Paris and rescue her son Chad, who has gone to the bad in that appropriate city. The Newsomes are sound commercial people, who have made money over manufacturing a small article of domestic utility. Henry James never tells us what the small article is, and in

*"The Ambassadors."* From *Aspects of the Novel* by E. M. Forster. 

[1] There is a masterly analysis of *The Ambassadors* from another standpoint in *The Craft of Fiction.* [See pp. 37-46.]

a moment we shall understand why. Wells spits it out in *Tono Bungay,* Meredith reels it out in *Evan Harrington,* Trollope prescribes it freely for Miss Dunstable, but for James to indicate how his characters made their pile—it would not do. The article is somewhat ignoble and ludicrous—that is enough. If you choose to be coarse and daring and visualize it for yourself as, say, a button-hook, you can, but you do so at your own risk: the author remains uninvolved.

Well, whatever it is, Chad Newsome ought to come back and help make it, and Strether undertakes to fetch him. He has to be rescued from a life which is both immoral and unremunerative.

Strether is a typical James character—he recurs in nearly all the books and is an essential part of their construction. He is the observer who tries to influence the action, and who through his failure to do so gains extra opportunities for observation. And the other characters are such as an observer like Strether is capable of observing—through lenses procured from a rather too first class oculist. Everything is adjusted to his vision, yet he is not a quietist—no, that is the strength of the device; he takes us along with him, we move.

When he lands in England (and a landing is an exalted and enduring experience for James, it is as vital as Newgate for Defoe; poetry and life crowd round a landing): when Strether lands, though it is only old England, he begins to have doubts of his mission, which increase when he gets to Paris. For Chad Newsome, far from going to the bad, has improved; he is distinguished, he is so sure of himself that he can be kind and cordial to the man who has orders to fetch him away; his friends are exquisite, and as for "women in the case" whom his mother anticipated, there is no sign of them whatever. It is Paris that has enlarged and redeemed him—and how well Strether himself understands this!

> His greatest uneasiness seemed to peep at him out of the possible impression that almost any acceptance of Paris might give one's authority away. It hung before him this morning, the vast bright Babylon, like some huge iridescent object, a jewel brilliant and hard, in which parts were not to be discriminated nor differences comfortably marked. It twinkled and trembled and melted together, and what seemed all surface one moment seemed all depth the next. It was a

place of which, unmistakably, Chad was fond; wherefore if he, Strether, should like it too much, what on earth, with such a bond, would become of either of them?

Thus, exquisitely and firmly, James sets his atmosphere—Paris irradiates the book from end to end, it is an actor though always unembodied, it is a scale by which human sensibility can be measured, and when we have finished the novel and allow its incidents to blur that we may see the pattern plainer, it is Paris that gleams at the center of the hour-glass shape—Paris—nothing so crude as good or evil. Strether sees this, and sees that Chad sees it, and when this stage is reached the novel takes a turn: there is, after all, a woman in the case; behind Paris, interpreting it for Chad, is the adorable and exalted figure of Mme de Vionnet. It is now impossible for Strether to proceed. All that is noble and refined in life concentrates in Mme de Vionnet and is reinforced by her pathos. She asks him not to take Chad away. He promises—without reluctance, for his own heart has already shown him as much—and he remains in Paris not to fight it but to fight for it.

For the second batch of ambassadors now arrives from the New World. Mrs. Newsome, incensed and puzzled by the unseemly delay, has despatched Chad's sister, his brother-in-law, and Mamie, the girl whom he is supposed to marry. The novel now becomes, within its ordained limits, most amusing. There is a superb set-to between the sister and Mme de Vionnet, while as for Mamie—here is Mamie, seen through Strether's eyes.

As a child, as a "bud," and then again as a flower of expansion, Mamie had bloomed for him, freely, in the almost incessantly open doorways of home; where he remembered her as first very forward, as then very backward—for he had carried on at one period, in Mrs. Newsome's parlours . . . a course of English Literature reinforced by exams and teas—and once more, finally, as very much in advance. But he had kept no great sense of points of contact; it not being in the nature of things at Woollett that the freshest of the buds should find herself in the same basket with the most withered of the winter apples. . . . he none the less felt, as he sat with the charming girl, the signal growth of a confidence. For she *was* charming, when all was said—and none the less so for the visible habit and practice of freedom and fluency. She was charming, he was aware, in spite of the fact that if he hadn't found her so he would have found her something he

> should have been in peril of expressing as "funny." Yes, she was funny, wonderful Mamie, and without dreaming it; she was bland, she was bridal—with never, that he could make out as yet, a bridegroom to support it; she was handsome and portly, and easy and chatty, soft and sweet and almost disconcertingly reassuring. She was dressed, if we might so far discriminate, less as a young lady than as an old one—had an old one been supposable to Strether as so committed to vanity; the complexities of her hair missed moreover also the looseness of youth; and she had a mature manner of bending a little, as to encourage and reward, while she held neatly in front of her a pair of strikingly polished hands: the combination of all of which kept up about her the glamour of her "receiving," placed her again perpetually between the windows and within sound of the ice cream plates, suggested the enumeration of all the names . . . gregarious specimens of a single type, she was happy to "meet."

Mamie is another Henry James type; nearly every novel contains her—Mrs. Gereth in *The Spoils of Poynton* for instance, or Henrietta Stackpole in *The Portrait of a Lady*. He is so good at indicating instantaneously and constantly that a character is second rate, deficient in sensitiveness, abounding in the wrong sort of worldliness; he gives such characters so much vitality that their absurdity is delightful.

So Strether changes sides and loses all hopes of marrying Mrs. Newsome. Paris is winning—and then he catches sight of something new. Is not Chad, as regards any fineness in him, played out? Is not Chad's Paris after all just a place for a spree? This fear is confirmed. He goes for a solitary country walk, and at the end of the day he comes across Chad and Mme de Vionnet. They are in a boat, they pretend not to see him, because their relation is at bottom an ordinary liaison, and they are ashamed. They were hoping for a secret weekend at an inn while their passion survived; for it will not survive, Chad will tire of the exquisite Frenchwoman, she is part of his fling; he will go back to his mother and make the little domestic article and marry Mamie. They know all this, and it is revealed to Strether though they try to hide it; they lie, they are vulgar—even Mme de Vionnet, even her pathos, is stained with commonness.

> It was like a chill in the air to him, it was almost appalling, that a creature so fine could be, by mysterious forces, a creature so exploited. For, at the end of all things, they *were* mysterious; she had

> but made Chad what he was—so why could she think she had made him infinite? She had made him better, she had made him best, she had made him anything one would; but it came to our friend with supreme queerness that he was none the less only Chad. . . . The work, however admirable, was nevertheless of the strict human order, and in short it was marvellous that the companion of mere earthly joys, of comforts, aberrations (however one classed them) within the common experience, should be so transcendently prized. . . . She was older for him to-night, visibly less exempt from the touch of time; but she was as much as ever the finest and subtlest creature, the happiest apparition, it had been given him, in all his years, to meet; and yet he could see her there as vulgarly troubled, in very truth, as a maidservant crying for a young man. The only thing was that she judged herself as the maidservant wouldn't; the weakness of which wisdom too, the dishonour of which judgment, seemed but to sink her lower.

So Strether loses them too. As he says: "I have lost everything—it is my only logic." It is not that they have gone back. It is that he has gone on. The Paris they revealed to him—he could reveal it to them now, if they had eyes to see, for it is something finer than they could ever notice for themselves, and his imagination has more spiritual value than their youth. The pattern of the hour-glass is complete; he and Chad have changed places, with more subtle steps than Thaïs and Paphnuce, and the light in the clouds proceeds not from the well-lit Alexandria, but from the jewel which "twinkled and trembled and melted together, and what seemed all surface one moment seemed all depth the next."

The beauty that suffuses *The Ambassadors* is the reward due to a fine artist for hard work. James knew exactly what he wanted, he pursued the narrow path of aesthetic duty, and success to the full extent of his possibilities has crowned him. The pattern has woven itself, with modulation and reservations Anatole France will never attain. But at what sacrifice!

So enormous is the sacrifice that many readers cannot get interested in James, although they can follow what he says (his difficulty has been much exaggerated), and can appreciate his effects. They cannot grant his premise, which is that most of human life has to disappear before he can do us a novel.

He has, in the first place, a very short list of characters. I have already mentioned two—the observer who tries to influence the action, and the second-rate outsider (to whom, for example, all the brilliant opening of *What Maisie Knew* is entrusted). Then there is the sympathetic foil—very lively and frequently female—in *The Ambassadors*—Maria Gostrey plays this part; there is the wonderful rare heroine, whom Mme de Vionnet approached and who is consummated by Milly in *The Wings of the Dove*; there is sometimes a villain, sometimes a young artist with generous impulses; and that is about all. For so fine a novelist it is a poor show.

In the second place, the characters, besides being few in number, are constructed on very stingy lines. They are incapable of fun, of rapid motion, of carnality, and of nine-tenths of heroism. Their clothes will not take off, the diseases that ravage them are anonymous, like the sources of their income, their servants are noiseless or resemble themselves, no social explanation of the world we know is possible for them, for there are no stupid people in their world, no barriers of language, and no poor. Even their sensations are limited. They can land in Europe and look at works of art and at each other, but that is all. Maimed creatures can alone breathe in Henry James's pages—maimed yet specialized. They remind one of the exquisite deformities who haunted Egyptian art in the reign of Akhnaton—huge heads and tiny legs, but nevertheless charming. In the following reign they disappear.

Now this drastic curtailment, both of the numbers of human beings and of their attributes, is in the interests of the pattern. The longer James worked, the more convinced he grew that a novel should be a whole—not necessarily geometric like *The Ambassadors,* but it should accrete round a single topic, situation, gesture, which should accupy the characters and provide a plot, and should also fasten up the novel on the outside—catch its scattered statements in a net, make them cohere like a planet, and swing through the skies of memory. A pattern must emerge, and anything that emerged from the pattern must be pruned off as wanton distraction. Who so wanton as human beings? Put Tom Jones or Emma or even Mr. Casaubon into a Henry James book, and the book will burn to ashes, whereas we could put them into one another's books and only cause local inflammation. Only a Henry James character will suit, and though they are not dead—certain selected recesses of experience he explores very well—they are gutted of the common stuff that fills characters in other books, and ourselves. And this castrating is not in the interests of the Kingdom of Heaven, there is no philosophy in the novels, no religion (except an occasional touch of superstition), no prophecy, no benefit for the superhuman at all. It is for the sake of a particular aesthetic effect which is certainly gained, but at this heavy price. . . .

# The New Generation

*by William Troy*

It is perhaps another evidence of his genius that Henry James, like certain other great writers of the past, has come to mean something different to each of the successive literary generations that have taken up his work. What James meant to the readers of *Harper's* and the *Atlantic* in the Eighties and Nineties, what he meant to the generation of Mr. H. G. Wells, or to the generation of Mr. T. S. Eliot and Mr. Ezra Pound, was probably not any of the things that he means, or may come to mean, to the generation in which we are naturally much interested—the present one. So abundant are the implications of his work that he is capable of being read—or misread—to suit the needs of widely different classes of readers, of distinct periods of literary taste; capable also of being "used," in a very real sense, as Shakespeare was used by the German romantics of the eighteenth century, or as Baudelaire is now being used by a whole wing of contemporary French and American poets. Of what possible "use" in this sense may James prove to be to the present generation of novelists? What lesson may this formidable and often-disputed master offer to the inheritors of his craft in our time? If his example includes anything of value special to them, if his strength corresponds to any of their numerous weaknesses, he should be appropriated at once, reinstated in the direct current of our letters.

It happens, moreover, that James is in immediate need of some sort of reinstatement at the moment. He remains suspended in that

"The New Generation," by William Troy. (Originally entitled "Henry James and the Young Writers.") *The Bookman* (June 1931). Reprinted by permission of the estate of William Troy; Leonie A. Troy, Administratrix.

vague limbo of disrepute to which the last generation of Freudian critics so often consigned their victims. He is easily the most tolerated author of his size in modern literature. The elaborate execution which Mr. Van Wyck Brooks performed in *The Pilgrimage of Henry James* was simply the final blow in the long catastrophe of his reputation. For more than forty years James had been chiefly read by people who admired him for hardly any more palpable reason than the vague penumbra of gentility which surrounded his pages. The close of his life was rendered positively unhappy (as we know from his letters) by the ribald humors of a new order which dismissed him as nothing short of a pompous old fool. Mr. Wells's brutal parody in *Boon* served to lay the ghost for prewar England. All that remained for Mr. Brooks in 1925 was to dispose of James in a more comprehensive fashion and in terms that should be more effective for the period. What Mr. Brooks did to James's reputation, however, is important, for the semi-ridiculous, semi-tragic figure that he created is the most popular conception of him at the moment.

For Mr. Brooks, it will be recalled, James offered nothing more nor less than a case history. Here was an example of an American who had sacrificed not only his promise as an artist but also his identity as an individual in the fruitless effort to adjust himself to an alien culture. All the habits of James's mind—"the caution, the ceremoniousness, the baffled curiosity, the nervousness and constant self-communion, the fear of committing himself"—are traceable to the long years he spent in England, where he had never been anything but "an enchanted exile in a museum world." A self-conscious guest in a house where he had never been at home, James reflected even in his style "the evasiveness, the hesitancy, the scrupulosity of an habitually embarrassed man." The diagnosis becomes steadily more emphatic toward the end. In James's later writings Mr. Brooks can discern no more than "the confused reveries of an invalid child." It is as if the author of *Roderick Hudson* and *The Portrait of a Lady* had developed at the last into a kind of "impassioned geometer—or, shall we say, some vast arachnid of art, pouncing upon the tiny air-blown particle and wrapping it round and round." What stands out most remarkably today in this analysis is a single statement which throws ever so much more light on Mr. Brooks than it does on Henry James: "What interested him (in his novels) was not the figures but their relations, the relations which alone make pawns significant."

To Mr. Brooks and his generation, as such a remark implies, an interest in relations was almost certain evidence of sterility in a writer. To concentrate on relations was to be faced immediately with the problems of value on which they hinged, and to betray an interest in any such problems was to be rendered more than a little suspect at the time. It was genuinely difficult for Mr. Brooks to conceive how a writer of James's manifest intelligence could have considered the relations of his "figures" more important than the movements of pawns in a game. It was difficult because it was almost impossible for his generation to recognize the existence of values or the part they usually play in vital literary creation. Even a game, it was forgotten, must have its rules; and for a game to be properly absorbing, for either player or spectator, the values assigned the rules must be accepted, temporarily at least, with something like seriousness. For James himself the rules did exist, and he accepted them with a passionate seriousness. Before ever they were apprehended by his mind, they were *felt,* and with enough intensity of feeling to provide the center, the very foundation of his artistic task. The "pawns" of his game, however inanimate they may sometimes seem in other respects, are always alive, even violently alive, in that portion of their being which James chose to explore and represent, because he believed it to be the richest and "most finely contributive" of all—the conscience.

By such a term as conscience one need not understand anything more definite than James himself ever intended by the term—that region of the mind, that area of our habitual mental activity, which is reserved for the recognition and solution of moral conflicts. At least to the extent that his "figures" do, every one of them, function in this region are they worthy of being called *characters*—or the label is without meaning. Often, it is true, the relations, situations, or patterns in which the somewhat special experience of their creator involves them are so unique or complex, so extremely tenuous, as to make them seem to respire a little outside the usual zone of verisimilitude. But the comparison with a geometer is inaccurate if it refers to anything but the hard and luminous detachment with which a given intellectual terrain is surveyed. For James the conscience that controlled the actions of his personages was something real and concrete; the values which determined for Fleda Vetch and Lambert Strether and Milly Theale the solution of their delicately attenuated problems were for him *true* values. For James's reader, however, who is primarily concerned with the interest that these problems afford, with their possible aesthetic result, there is no such obligation to accept these particular values as true. For him it is simply necessary to accept their reality in the minds of the characters, to imagine, if only for the time being, that they *might* be considered true, for the sake of the satisfaction that their representation provides in an orderly executed work of art.

For various reasons this was an effort of the imagination that few in the last generation showed themselves able or willing to make. Perhaps the chief reason was the particular psychological absolutism of the time, which submerged personality beneath that plane of conscious judgment which for James and others before him had constituted the real domain of character. The belief in character that had sustained James was not recognized because it was not understood; and his fervid explorations could only be explained as the mystifying vagaries of someone who had ventured too far outside the normal bounds of experience. He could be accounted for only as a kind of exquisite monster, as the victim of some fundamental lesion of personality or—as the critics would have it—as a psychological "case." The formula was ready at hand and it was rich in possibilities of embroidery. Everything in James's mind and work—his characters, his themes, his form and style even—became immediately clear when it was once remembered that he was an American who had spent most of his adult years in Europe.

Whatever truth there may be in this formula as applied to other native American writers who have forsworn their country for the warm securities of European culture, one may question its validity as a total explanation of all that characterized Henry James as a man and an artist. Some of the more superficial biases of his mind, some of the minor idiosyncrasies of his style, can doubtless be traced to the influence of his prolonged residence in England. But one might show the equivalent consequences on his contemporary, William Dean Howells, of a migration from Ohio to Boston at about the same period. Unquestionably also, in his choice of backgrounds, characters, and the situations in which he placed them, James was affected for better or worse by the particular foreign milieu in which he happened to pass the greater part of his life. If certain subjects, like that of American "innocence" caught in the toils of European duplicity, recur constantly throughout his work it is merely because these subjects repeated themselves so often in the course of his experience, and therefore became the most familiar patterns of reality available to him. To complain of these subjects, however, on the grounds that they are too narrow, or too special, or too refined, is illegitimate. It is to decline to play what James himself called "the fair critical game with an author," which is to grant him his postulates. "His subject is what is given him—given him by influences, by a process, with which we have nothing to do; since what art, what revelation, can ever really make such a mystery, such a passage as the private life of the intellect, adequately traceable for us? His treatment of it, on the other hand, is what he actively gives; and it is with what he gives that we are critically concerned."

Behind and above everything else was Henry James's mind, with its special quality, endowment and direction. What is all too seldom realized, for it would alone discredit Mr. Brooks's thesis, is that the main set and direction of that mind was already well established long before James ever made his decision to settle in England. Already he had formulated, in a review of Walt Whitman written in 1865, what was to be the principle of his artistic creed for the whole of his career: "To be positive, one must have something to say; to be positive requires reason, labor, and art; and art requires above all things a suppression of one's self to an idea." The real problem before him in those early wander-years was not the quest of some place that might change or modify the native bent of his mind, but one that should offer to his mind greater opportunities for play, a richer field in which to grow and expand, a more *plausible* background for the working out of his particular "idea." It was a problem of nutrition. And it was only after a trial-and-error process—for there was the important experiment of his year in Paris—that he hit upon the country that seemed most suitable to his purpose.

It might quite as easily be shown that the truth is the exact opposite of what Mr. Brooks and others have contended: that for James residence in England, rather than being a source of sterility and corruption, was an indispensable condition of fulfillment. Since these critics had made up their minds not to occupy themselves with his work, with what as an artist he had "given," they might equally well have considered the reverse of the medal: What would have happened to James if he had turned to the society that awaited him in the Boston or New York of the late nineteenth century? Would James, with his peculiarly refined sensibility, have escaped an ordeal less intense than that which Mr. Brooks has elsewhere traced in the career of Mark Twain? Indeed, there was hardly any means of salvation for the artist in Mr. Brooks's scheme of nineteenth century America. Upon further reflection Mr. Brooks might well have concluded that in one sense there is never any salvation for the artist—at any time or in any place. His only chance of fulfillment is to be as good an artist as he can under the conditions of his time and the limitations of his own temperament. But such a view would lead instantly to an entirely different kind of criticism. One would have to concentrate more directly on the study and evaluation of a writer's work.

## II

The specific question which we set out to examine was in what sense and to what extent may James's example have any special meaning for the novelists of our generation. How, we may inquire, may he show them the way to make their work more deeply and broadly *interesting?*

For the sole obligation of the novel, its one excuse for being, as James insisted, is that it be interesting. The question which such a demand leaves in the mind is, of course, what, properly speaking, constitutes the interest of a novel? Fortunately, in his essays, prefaces and letters James has provided us with a complete and lucid exposition of his own view of the problem. There is life obviously, which is the novel-writer's material, and there is art, which consists of the special use that he makes of his material. Life is common, inexhaustible, chaotic—a "splendid waste," to use James's fine phrase.

It is art alone that gives it beauty and meaning, through the form and expression with which the creative mind endows it, for "expression is creation and makes the reality." To be interesting, therefore, a novel must give or lend something to the "splendid waste" which is life. That something is "composition," the design which the artist makes out of the scattered and unchecked flow of his impressions and responses. Without such design the novel would have no identity as an art form, no value as a projection of reality, and hence no meaning to the mind or the imagination. "I hold that interest may be, *must be,* exquisitely made and created, and that if we don't make it, we who undertake to, nobody and nothing will make it for us," James wrote to Wells at the close of his life. And in the same letter he makes an even more complete avowal of his belief in the unique and absolute value of the artistic process: "It is art that *makes* life, makes importance, for our consideration and application of these things, and I know of no substitute whatever for the force and beauty of its process."

The various alternatives to this view of the novelist's special role and function are necessarily vague and contradictory. There are for example the exponents of "life"—of life *tout court,* of life at any cost. What precisely, however, do these people mean? If the novel is to be classified at all it is as an art form, and if art means anything it means the process by which the materials of life are arranged and fused into a unity. It is only through its unity that the meaning and value of a given work of art are to be discovered. A novel with insufficient evidence of unity represents mere arbitrariness, or ineptitude, or the surrender of the mind to the rich disorder of nature. It is possible, James admitted, to reproduce life—its substance and even its quality, its imponderable multiplicity—but without art ("composition") the result would be devoid of meaning. "There may in its absence be life, incontestably, as *The Newcomes* has life, as *Les Trois Mousquetaires,* as Tolstoy's *War and Peace* have it; but what do such large loose baggy monsters, with their queer elements of the accidental and the arbitrary, artistically *mean.* . . . There is life and life, and as waste is only life sacrificed and thereby prevented from 'counting,' I delight in a deep-breathing economy and an organic form."

Yet it would be wholly wrong to interpret such a statement as merely another expression of the "art for art's sake" doctrine which was so loudly articulate in James's own lifetime and to which he objected from the beginning. While James was firm in his recognition of aesthetic values he was definitely not an aesthete—that is to say, one for whom the means is also the end. For James even the patterns of art owe their initial suggestion to reality. Even composition depends on the existence of elements already present in life, elements capable of being drawn together with greater tightness, concentration and beauty through the artistic process. Form is not therefore something distinct from life, but the arrangement of something already there, or at least there for the artist's specially trained observation. Unlike the real aesthete, James distrusted all constructions of the mind which did not derive their parallel somewhere in experience. "Never can a composition of this sort," he writes of *The Ambassadors,* "have sprung straighter from a dropped grain of suggestion, and never can that grain, developed, overgrown and smothered, have yet lurked more in the mass as an independent particle." And surely *The Ambassadors* is a good enough example of his later more complex and "geometrical" style! Whatever were the limitations of his experience his brain was never, like Mallarmé's for example, haunted by the memory of azure skies shut out, never drained of content

*Comme le pot de fard gisant au pied d'un mur.*

But what, since we have only mentioned them, are the elements of those patterns which life is made to assume in the imagination of the artist? Since they can be observed they must be objective; and objective patterns of human life can be built on one thing only, action. Action, to James, is therefore the "soul of the novel." All else is subordinate—description, "local color," incidental ideas, everything in fact not strictly related to the progressive explication of the central narrative core. At the same time the highest interest cannot be created by action alone, that is, action considered for its own sake. If incident is the illustration of character, character itself is the determination of incident. What is always really interesting is character and that can only be fully understood through an imaginative reconstruction of the motives that precede action in the mind. The external patterns of life—and this is commonplace enough—have significance only in so far as we are made acquainted with the complex and never to be wholly apprehended background of motives behind them.

The moment we speak of motives we are headed straight into the whole field of difficulties whose attempted solution afforded the passion of James's task as an imaginative artist. These are, in a word, all those difficulties which are set up by the necessity of the individual to adjust himself to some moral order. The most interesting patterns of art are in fact just those that the novelist is able to construct out of the often wasted, unrealized possibilities thrown up by these predicaments in life. Motives exist in all their confused and multiple variety; sometimes, but rarely, they fall into design of their own accord; it is the novelist's special business to see that what is thus accidental is always achieved. His business is with the motives behind conduct because they are what make fiction, as they make life, difficult—and, so, interesting. For that reason James exclaimed at "the moral timidity of the usual English novelist, with his (or with her) aversion to face the difficulties with which on every side the treatment of reality bristles." To shun these difficulties was in fact to miss the peculiar excitement on which, in the last analysis, everything depended.

To imply solution of any absolute sort is of course to assume a standard, a criterion to which in the end all problems may be referred. Here it will have to be enough to say that by a moral order James understood some body of felt values existing through one or another process of absorption in the individual's mind. For the individual's adjustment to be imperative these values must not only exist, but exist in a strong and potent way. Without this assumption of values as something felt one cannot make the assumption of art; for one cannot otherwise account for the extreme intensity of those conflicts around which the fiction artist erects his constructions. Nor can one explain the quite real importance which these imagined conflicts take on in the reader's interest. Against some background of felt values, therefore, every individual conflict must be set; and on some such individual conflict the scheme of every novel must rest.

In these terms, plot, for example, becomes more easily definable:

it is the abstract curve of the moral drama being enacted in the mind or conscience of a character. It is quantitatively all that development, growth and expansion of "the dropped grain of suggestion" which has excited in the first place the novelist's passion for difficulties. In the same way, it may be seen how aesthetic values are necessarily subordinated to other values anterior to them in reality. Subordinated is perhaps hardly the word—for the two kinds of values are really so identified as to be altogether indistinguishable. The aesthetic pattern *is* the moral pattern—or the beginning, middle and end of all that has taken place in the active conscience of the individual.

## III

Unlike almost all of his fellow novelists in English, James served a deliberate apprenticeship during which he learned everything he could about the nature and function of his craft. Before writing as he did write (for, once established, his style and method progressed only in refinement) he had surveyed the field, measured the hazards, and envisaged all the possible alternatives. In his own lifetime he had the opportunity to study all the later mutations of the novel form—the English Victorians (with their "fluid puddings") and the Russians, French realism and naturalism, and two whole epochs of pure aestheticism. During his memorable year in France he learned so much about what the novel as novel might be that a contemporary French critic like M. Gide finds his work too much in the native tradition to captivate his taste. But he also learned, from Flaubert especially, the ultimate emptiness of even the most perfect work of art that pretended to an absolute moral indifference. From the Goncourts he learned that mere *décor,* no matter how sumptuous, was a poor substitute indeed for motivated human action. (thus, years afterwards, writing *The Spoils of Poynton,* he avoids offering any detailed description of the furniture and other objects which are actually the source of the drama.) Most of all, from Zola he learned that art and science were two different quantities, and that art at least was a quantity that was not to be amassed through perspiration alone. Of the group as a whole his indictment is significant: "The conviction that held them together was the conviction that art and morality are two perfectly different things and that the former has no more to do with the latter than it has with astronomy or embryology."

Because he had eliminated all these alternatives James may be said to have escaped all the blunders and excesses to which the novel after him was condemned. He himself could hardly have foreseen that so long after his pointed remark about Zola—"if he had as much light as energy, his results would be of the highest value"—the same process of burrowing in the dark would be resumed by Mr. Theodore Dreiser. Hardly less could he have guessed that aestheticism would one day fade away into the pallid *fabliaux* of Mr. James Branch Cabell and the variegated pastiche of Mr. Thornton Wilder. But he must certainly have realized that naturalism carried far enough was bound to result in a subjectivism that should be opposed by its very nature to the traditions of an ordered art. He was certainly aware that to desert the living world of action was to descend to a region where anything resembling order was impossible. Did he not refer to impressionism like that of D'Annunzio as "the open door to the trivial"? Impressionism in our day is called by a different name but the Jamesian objection is still valid. Psychoanalysis in fiction is simply impressionism supported by a method; and impressionism in the novel has meant the same abandonment of character at the level where its possibilities for the artist are most interesting. For James as an artist, order, the assumption of order, was essential; and to submerge beneath the plane where order was possible was merely to renounce one's aspirations to the primordial chaos, to become lost in the "splendid waste."

The real difficulty in our time has of course been values. The old ones are no longer capable of generating enough conviction in actual living to justify their continued representation in fiction, the new have been found uniformly insufficient. Here, it must be granted, James can hardly be expected to offer any more immediate succor than has been thus far offered by contemporary life. But as he has already revealed the necessity and the exact function of values in narrative art he can now do much to prevent a certain confusion in regard to the novelist's proper relation to them.

Nothing in James's own example or declaration, let it be said, allows us to understand that it is ever the business of the novelist to establish values. As he assumed them from the society of the period in which he lived, so must those who follow after him in the path of the novel assume them from the moral consciousness of their own time. The contemporary writer can only hope to discover in the complex welter of our time those standards of judgment which emerge with sufficient strength and frequency to stand the test of being submitted to the artistic process. He must search, observe, experiment, and then make his test with the almost certain prospect of defeat for a considerable time to come. It may be that for some years he will have to be content to operate without nearly so cohesive a body of felt values as obtained in the past. He may be compelled to devote himself to the paid atrophy and decline of those values in the present; to the issues caused by their dramatic refusal to be displaced; or to the equally dramatic effort of those new values which shall gradually assert themselves in the future. Any one of these courses would be more truly creative, according to the Jamesian point of view, than the blind appropriation of values which are no longer felt because they are no longer sufficiently alive.

## IV

What the writers of our time can learn from James is not anything distinctly represented in his achievement; nothing implicit in his style or method, which are both too personal ever to be duplicated; not his "philosophy," not even the assumptions about human character which were for him the source of so much eloquence. What they can learn from him is the deepest meaning of the phrase "the integrity of the artist." He can show them to what an essential degree the artist is dependent on something anterior to himself in life; how the truest values of art are never to be dissociated from the most potent values of the world about him; and how, although the particular values of the one are always in one sense relative to those of the other, the single constant in the whole relationship is the fact of the artistic impulse. And as a last check on the possible interpretation that all this implies a certain dangerous relativity of values for art, he has written: "There is one point at which the moral sense and the artistic sense lie very close together; that is in the light of the very obvious truth that the deepest quality of a work of art will always be the quality of the mind of the producer . . . that seems to me an axiom which, for the artist in fiction, will cover all needful moral ground."

# The Essential Novelist?

*by Pelham Edgar*

There is no question here of a rehabilitation of Henry James. He is, to be sure, at the moment more taken for granted than read, but his reputation is for all that secure, and he holds the anomalous position, in spite of all neglect, of being in a formative way the most important novelist of his time. What he lacks and what he possesses we may now all too briefly examine.

Some of the objections against his work are generalizations without point or depth. Mr. Van Wyck Brooks, for example, in his *Pilgrimage of Henry James* elaborates the specious argument that a writer who abandons his country is invariably shorn of his strength. Hardy, we might agree, would not have written so convincingly if he had shifted his base to Scotland or America, but the material in which James worked could not be found concentrated in a hundred square miles of heath and meadow. There were rare moments in which he felt that he had not adequately nourished his genius, as we may gather from a letter to his brother William cautioning him to guard his children against the dangers of the uprooted state and urging him to permit them "to contract local saturations and attachments in respect to their *own* great and glorious country, to learn, and strike roots into, its infinite beauty, as, I suppose, and variety. . . . Its being their own will double their *use* of it."

As a generalization we can admit the truth of Mr. Brooks's con-

"The Essential Novelist?" (Originally entitled "The Essential Novelist? Henry James.") From *The Art of the Novel* (New York: The Macmillan Company, 1933) by Pelham Edgar, pp. 172-183. 

tention that the home-keeping novelist has a better chance and possesses his material more securely than one who flees from his native responsibilities. But as a particularization for James's individual case the argument imperfectly applies. In the first place he was possessed of as much American material as he could absorb, and he confidently employed that limited amount. And again we must realize that a man's country is not always or necessarily the country of his birth. We must distinguish between our natural and our spiritual home, and every circumstance of the young James's upbringing turned his mind and inclinations Europewards. As he matured these affinities strengthened. What increasingly interested him were the developed forms of civilization, the rich accretions which time and tradition alone can give.

Civilization in the making is exciting, but that could never be peculiarly James's affair except as affording the artistic relief of contrasted types. So we may conclude that James followed the law of his own genius, and even if he never succeeded in taking the hue of his adopted surroundings he was the better fitted to instruct the Englishman or the Frenchman in aspects of their own civilization worth recording, but which by excess of familiarity had escaped their attention.

Mr. H. G. Wells's ascription of triviality to James demands a sharper protest, for it rests on a perverse misapprehension of the function of the novel. It is a form, we grant, that may be bent to many and legitimate uses, but the more you deviate from its essential conditions the more dangers you incur. If you work outwards from a core of human interest you can be argumentative, didactic, reformatory, sociological, and many things besides, but always at the peril of the artistic integrity of your process. James neglects these excrescent attachments of fiction, and concentrates all the powers of his intellect on the artistic presentation of human behavior under conditions designed to reveal character at the maximum of intensity that situations on the hither side of tragedy may bear. It is by virtue of these abstentions, and by his supreme concentration on the central interest that we venture to name him the "essential" novelist. His work is the most rigidly "canalized" we know, with never a leak in the firm cement of its masonry, and never a deviation in the mathematical directness of its flow. Such

Euclidean exactness is teasing to many readers, but while we can understand Mr. Wells's impatience at the supreme concentrative process of the novels and their apparent defect in general interest, we must again insist that their themes are of such importance as to escape his too casual imputation of triviality. At the worst he is occasionally more orotund and magnificent in manner than a slight occasion may warrant, wrapping a simple situation round with a bewildering web of words.

Other criticism have more sanction in the facts, for every author must have the defects of his qualities. The sheet must always be balanced, and if we get something in abundance we pay for it somewhere else. Thus if we have no stint of the refined subtleties that extreme culture provides, we may be prepared for a deficiency in the raw materials of human nature. Henry James, then, is accused of not being primitive enough, of doing scant justice for example to such elemental characters as abound in the novels of George Eliot and Hardy. Such characters are certainly not James's chosen field, and he would be ill at ease with a peasant or laborer on his hands; but a survey of his work will show that he is not utterly deficient in simple types, and that he occasionally "does" them well. They are merely not in his general scheme, any more than the sophisticated business man in his office, or the professional man at his desk. We find the business man bewilderedly roaming Europe, in which lost state he is sufficiently convincing, and there is the study of a professional man, Sir Luke Strett in *The Wings of the Dove,* that is one of the minor successes of the book. The objection then we shall let pass as a valid one, making merely the reservation that if elemental qualities are in question an author sufficiently skilled can discover them beneath all the obscuring folds of civilization. It is a more exacting problem, but James went far toward solving it.

It is in his later books that James imagined himself to have found his true direction. They were the fruit of prolonged observation and ceaseless concern for the art of presentation. But the subtlety which went to their making, and certain stylistic peculiarities which developed when Miss Bosanquet's typewriter[1] was substituted for his own pen, combined to limit the circle of his audience until

[1] Theodora Bosanquet was Henry James's amanuensis from 1908 to 1916.

ultimately his books became the delight only of the curious and courageous reader. His complaints on this ground are comical when they are not pathetic. He knew that his range of observation had widened, and that he had learned by repeated experimentation, so he fondly imagined, every technical device for revealing the latent values of a theme. But as his power grew his readers vanished, and this brings us to the very heart of the James problem. Is it possible, we ask ourselves, that a subject may be overworked? Does life leak out when art comes in, and will the novel of the future be lighter in its elaboration and more genially careless in its effects? I do not like to think so. I feel that the public has been too easily frightened, and that the last books are definitely and demonstrably finer than the first. But also we must realize that Henry James was a pioneer two hundred years after his art had been first established, and though there may be something stiff and constrained in his movements his successors may profit by his labors, and gain ease and freedom from his example.

No purpose would be served by dwelling on the early books which, save for the very earliest, are none the less delightful reading for being somewhat belatedly in the expiring romantic tradition. Transition dawned in *The Portrait of a Lady,* and deepened in *The Princess Casamassima.* After *The Tragic Muse* (1889) came a period when he confined himself to dramatic writing and the composition of short stories. It was during this season of abstention from major novel writing that his later theories of fiction germinated, and they find their first untrammeled manifestation in a half-length novel, *The Spoils of Poynton,* which appeared in 1896. From then onward he was almost painfully conscious of the effect he wished to produce and of the means of producing it. If this new discipline had entailed a loss of spontaneity we might well regret the change, but we find rather an increase of compositional ardor, and an inspirational glow that is lacking in the naïver works of his early prime. A further interest is engendered by the remarkable variety of method from book to book. A uniform style binds them together, but apart from their rhetoric each book is a new experiment in design. The cunning with which they are contrived demands closer attention than we are usually willing to bring to fiction. There are so many dodges that even with the commentary of the prefaces we are likely to miss not a few. Mr. Lubbock comes valiantly to our aid in his masterly analysis of *The Ambassadors.* For the other books we must rely unfortunately on our own more limited insight.

One of these, *The Wings of the Dove,* I propose to go into with some care. For some of the remainder I limit myself to the briefest annotation merely to indicate the variety of attack which differentiates them.

We know that James habitually found his incentive in a theme, and fitted his characters to his subject rather than the subject to the characters. One illustrative figure at the most might be a twin birth with the idea. The genesis of *The Spoils of Poynton* is known. A dinner-table conversation had given him the suggestion of a woman who in her husband's lifetime had made his house beautiful with objects that her taste had brought together, and who after his death faces the prospect of losing the things she loved by the marriage of her son with a girl who could not value them. I can think of no other novelist who would have been thrilled with the possibilities of such a theme, but it entered James's imagination and he achieved a minor masterpiece.

We shall not follow all the steps by which it grew. It is sufficient to say that he rejected the subsequent detail which life provided in this particular instance, and allowed himself to be swayed by what he regarded as the superior logic of the imagination. His task was to create the world of people, and the smaller and more workable this world the better, that might allow the idea its unimpeded growth. Mrs. Gereth's identity once firmly established necessitated the inevitable kind of son and prospective daughter-in-law to complicate the action. But it was when he had discovered Fleda Vetch that the supreme precipitation of all the elements was possible. Everything now becomes drama reflected through her personality, and she blessedly permits the author to retreat into his inscrutable background. It was under such impersonal conditions that James's creative imagination most liberally worked, and these were to be the law of all his future compositions.

To organize a theme round some pivotal center, to find the requisite balance for all its conflicting forces and by a skillful distribution of emphasis to reveal the harmony that lies at the heart of complexity, these are preoccupations which can be exhibited only on a miniature scale within the brief compass of *The Spoils of Poynton,* and the next half-length novel, *What Maisie Knew,* is only another short step forward in the main direction. We find more to our purpose in *The Awkward Age* the deft workmanship of which even James has not surpassed.

The book was something in the nature of a challenge. Some of his converted dramas, *The Outcry* and *The Other House* we may instance, fell naturally into the conversational mold. We may entertain the view that every subject has its appropriate form of presentation, but *The Awkward Age* was cast in dialogue mainly because James was dissatisfied with the disordered way in which dialogue was employed in current fiction. There seemed no inevitable reason other than this for his choice of the scenic method. He had always maintained the high virtue of dialogue. It is the novelist's main dramatic resource, but its highest effect is gained when it is prepared by all the devices which the novelist, unlike the dramatist, has at his disposal. He was now determined to prove that speech even deprived of these supports is competent to bear the whole weight of the action, and he chose a drawing-room comedy as his testing medium. His success was indeed extraordinary. It would not be correct to say that there is no deviation from dialogue. There are brilliant thumbnail sketches identifying the characters, but except for these there is nothing but speech—no narrative, no description beyond the barest indication, no analysis, and no general reflection. Yet the story gets itself in movement, and the characters develop themselves in sharpest outline. James felt that he had never surpassed the presentation of Mrs. Brookenham. The general reader is perhaps more impressed by Nanda, and is as fully seized of the characters of Mr. Longdon, Vanderbank, the Duchess, and Mitchy. In sheer cleverness James has never surpassed this sparkling ironic comedy, but it is doubtful if he has profited by his own example, for the dialogue of his later books, fine though it is, has not the same liveliness or revealing quality.

We must beware of regarding James as a mathematician delighting only in pure form. He cultivates form always in the interest of substance, holding it as an affair of conscience that his human material should have the finest rendering that art can contrive. There is always an interblending of the two aspects, and his meaning is missed when we fail to grasp this fusion. If I have emphasized the formal element in James it is because he valued its heightening possibilities more than any of his contemporaries, who are so often artists as it were by accident. But the human values we must never slight, and one might hazard the opinion that if James had been endowed with a richer sense of life he would have been incomparably the greatest novelist who ever lived. What we have is fine enough to be thankful for, and in a relative way we may say that he has made the fullest use of the gifts he possessed.

And these gifts on the human side are not small. He did not touch life on so many sides as others one might name, but his perceptions within their limitations are still very fine and true. He has not more humor than would fill his sails with the gentlest breeze, but there is in him a blending of tenderness and irony that is almost unique in our literature, so rarely do these two qualities coexist. *The Awkward Age* and *What Maisie Knew* exhibit this combination to perfection, but not more perfectly than *The Wings of the Dove* to which we now turn.

Here the tenderness is provided for in the circumstance of James's personal experience. His life abounded in friendships, but whether he was capable or not of the intensities of passion still the woman once existed whom he might have loved. It was his cousin Mary Temple, whom in his caressing retrospective way he commemorates in his autobiographical memoir, and whom he revives for us in the tragic figure of Mildred Theale.

> She was absolutely afraid of nothing she might come to by living with enough sincerity and enough wonder; and I think it is because one was to see her launched on that adventure in such bedimmed, such almost tragically compromised conditions, that one is caught by her title to the heroic and pathetic mark. . . . One may have wondered rather doubtingly what life would have had for her, and how her exquisite faculty of challenge could have worked in with what she was likely otherwise to have encountered or been confined to. None the less did she in fact cling to consciousness; death, at the last, was dreadful to her; she would have given anything to live—and the image of this, which was long to remain with me, appeared so of the essence of tragedy that I was in the far-off aftertime to seek to lay the ghost by wrapping it, a particular occasion aiding, in the beauty and dignity of art.

So much for the tenderness. What humor there is flows entirely from Mrs. Lowder whose ponderous effectiveness is lightly rendered. But the hilarity is not excessive, and the irony is withheld until the closing pages when Kate touches the triumph of her treachery to find Milly's pale ghost rising between her and the consummation of her desire.

I have not yet discussed style in its rhetorical aspect. With James this would be a grave omission, for with respect to the choice and manipulation of words, and in the harmonious fall of his periods he is a sufficient master. In qualities of actual writing he bears it away from all his rivals. He is consistently finer than Meredith or Hardy, and there are in him more pages that we dwell on for the sheer beauty of the expression. Infelicities there are of course, but these are mainly constructional, such as his multiplied parentheses, and a mannerism that grew upon him of willfully misplacing his prepositions. It would require an expert grammarian to analyze the following sentence from *The Wings of the Dove*:

> It was the handsome girl alone, one of his own species and his own society, who had made him feel uncertain; of his certainties about a mere little American, a cheap exotic, imported almost wholesale and whose habitat, with its conditions of climate, growth and cultivation, its immense profusion but its few varieties and their development, he was perfectly satisfied.

There is perhaps nothing more radically wrong in this sentence than a mere suspended meaning. But there is no need to multiply these trifling but teasing peculiarities. His greatness as a writer stands out the more prominently because alone among his contemporaries he had the courage of length. There is a conspiracy of brevity among our writers, and whatever value for beauty there is in the sustained period we have lost. When James is at his best the great wash of his words flows like a tide into all the emotional recesses of his subject, and we are willing then to forgive the occasional heaviness and the not infrequent overelaboration.

*The Wings of the Dove* has as much of this verbal music as any of his novels, and the construction of the fable, though less subtle and successful than he had hoped, bears every evidence of the accustomed Jamesian care. The focal center of the book is obviously the exposition of Milly Theale's predicament. What are the difficulties to be encountered, and what the best ways of circumventing them? She is to be made delicate, because it is of the essence of the book that life shall elude her, and rich and sensitive because she must have at her command all the possibilities that life can offer. Experiences must be invented to reveal her qualities, and characters devised to generate these experiences and reflect her influence.

These conditions James readily enough fulfilled, but he "got off" as we say to a brilliant but disastrous start, if a proportional distribution of interest was to be attained. In other words, he built up the Kate Croy and Densher background so elaborately that he did not leave himself sufficient space to move round in the crucial second half of his book. And apart from this loss of the true perspective, he ran the risk of establishing two centers where one was intended. He has therefore to labor very hard to keep Milly Theale in the foreground of our interest, and that he has succeeded is as great a tribute to his manipulative skill as his triumph in *The Ambassadors* where his original plan required no such rectification. Mildred Theale will stand no rough handling, and her creator's solicitude keeps us perhaps at too respectful a distance from her, as the strong arm of the law restrains the curious crowd from too close an approach to the royal presence. He is always remembering and applying the Polonius dictum "by indirection to find direction out." To Mrs. Humphry Ward he wrote of "that magnificent and masterly *indirectness* which means the only dramatic straightness and intensity." And again to Mrs. Ward with particular reference to the present book:

> I note how again and again I go but a little way with the direct—that is, with the straight—exhibition of Milly; it resorts for relief, this process, wherever it can, to some kinder, some merciful indirection; all as if to approach her circuitously, deal with her at second hand, as an unspotted princess is ever dealt with; the pressure all round her kept easy for her, the sounds, the movements regulated, the forms and ambiguities made charming. All of which proceeds, obviously, from her painter's tenderness of imagination about her, which reduced him to watching her, as it were, through the successive windows of other people's interest in her.

This process of indirection is not new with James. He had practiced it before in his presentation of the Princess Casamassima. But he is now more confirmed in his use of the method and in his belief in its efficacy. It entails certain sacrifices. We cannot inhabit the mind of a character so treated. Only twice in the book—at Mrs. Lowder's first dinner party, and after the second visit to Sir Luke Strett—are we permitted to participate at any length in the operations of Milly's consciousness, and our participations even in her conversations are but sparsely conceded. James has obtained an effect, but whether the greatest possible I am not convinced. Mr. Galsworthy has accorded the same treatment to Irene Forsyte, but she is not central in his picture. "Successive windows" are all very well, but we feel ourselves somehow cheated of the great scene when Densher visits the dying girl, and we are granted only the pallid after-report of the interview. Of all the Jamesian innovations this is the most questionable.

# The Contemporary Subject

*by Stephen Spender*

The question for a writer of our time, which is at the back of all the discussed questions of belief, and of contemporary sensibility, is what is the modern subject? A subject large enough to enable the poet to write long poems, to make possible a dramatic poetry. To free the novel from mere *rapportage* or case history, and yet to relate it to the political life, the morality and manners of the time.

To say that *The Waste Land* "effects a complete severance between poetry and belief" is in itself almost meaningless: what is more explicit is, I think, to say that *The Waste Land* is an example of a long poem without any subject, or in so far as there is any subject, it is the conscious lack of belief, to which I. A. Richards has drawn attention. What we are offered instead of a subject is a pattern of diverse impressions: instead of any statement about life or the universe having been made, a kind of historic order has been achieved when the author says, "These fragments I have shored against my ruins." We are aware of his sense of our unenviable position in the history of our civilization, and of a vast background.

What a writer writes about is related to what he believes. What he writes about also implies an attitude to the time in which he is living. It is here that I. A. Richards' doctrine of "severance" comes in. For if there is conflict between the belief of the man and the belief of the time in which he is living, the belief that should

"The Contemporary Subject." (Originally entitled "Henry James and the Contemporary Subject.") Chapter Ten of *The Destructive Element* by Stephen Spender. Reprinted by permission of Jonathan Cape, Ltd.

be positive in the man is turned negative, in its reaction to his contemporaries. In such a situation, there are various courses open to a writer. He may escape entirely from his surroundings; into the past, into the country. The poetry of Walter de la Mare is today an example at its most interesting of that kind of an escape into an unreal world: some of the poetry of W. H. Davies an example of escape at its most facile. The writer may, on the other hand, try and justify his own position by "shoring up his fragments," and postulating an entire world of unbelief around him. This is what produces the appearance of a "severance between poetry and belief." But, of course, the writer of *The Waste Land* himself believes. He believes in the part of London where

> the walls
> Of Magnus Martyr hold
> Inexplicable splendour of Ionian white and gold.

What he is chiefly implying, though, is that in other, dead generations, there was a tradition of belief to which he could doubtless have conformed. What he is now implying is that he is living in a time of disbelief. What he is doubting is the efficacy and the value of his own private beliefs.

When I speak of writers who have beliefs, I am now discussing writers whose subjects are moral, or, in the widest sense, political, and I am not thinking of "pure" artists. I have chosen the writers in this book, because they are political-moral artists who are in the dilemma of Hamlet: they find their lives fixed in a world in which there are no external symbols for their inner sense of values. There is no power, and no glory. They are, therefore, forced either to satirize the world by showing it up as it really is (you may call such satire amoral, if you like, but to do so, as I hope to show, is a confusion) or they are obliged to try and reconcile the world with themselves, by adopting a hopeful evangelizing tone, or they are obliged to invent a set of symbols of their own, and, in the eyes of the world, like Hamlet, to feign madness; or they may retreat into the realms of pure art. The generation of Henry James, in a tradition carried on through Joyce, Wyndham Lewis, and Ezra Pound, produced a whole series of long (in some cases "unfinished symphonies"), excellent and unreadable masterpieces, full of moral feeling, but a moral feeling that is not satisfactorily illustrated by the subject.

I now turn to James, because one sees in his writing, as on a very large-scale map, the course of a great deal of modern literature.

Most criticism of James boils down to saying that he is unreadable. This is a very reasonable complaint, and one that a critic should certainly discuss. But I have tried to show that his unreadability has been attributed to the wrong causes—to his snobbishness, his prudery, and the difficulties of his style.

His method of presentation is, indeed, a sufficient reason for his not becoming a popular classic, in the Dickensian sense; but so far is it from being the real error that makes the neglect of him in a sense justified, it is his greatest contribution to the novel as a form.

What James did in fact revolutionize is the manner of presenting the scene in the novel: and the relation of the described scene to the emotional development of the characters. The novel has, of course, in the presentation of the passions, never broken quite away from the tradition of the theater: in Balzac, in Flaubert, in Tolstoy, in Dickens, in Thackeray, the reflective and descriptive and philosophic parts of the books are all threads connecting us with certain dramatic scenes, which are, in particular, of the greatest emotional importance. In the description, we see the alignment of characters; in the scenes we witness the release of emotions, the expression of passion.

In Joyce, in Proust, in James, this process is reversed. The scene, with accompanying dialogue and action, is used mainly as a means of aligning the characters: explaining what are the reactions of each to the other, what each reflects, and bringing characters together. The descriptive parts of the book, which are mainly monologues, are used to reveal the growth of passionate feelings, of love, of hatred. There are, of course, scenes which are highly dramatic, but the emphasis of these is not revelatory: they are the climax of what has already been revealed. When Fanny Assingham smashes the golden bowl, we know exactly what she and Maggie think of the bowl as a symbol of all the passionate feelings which are associated with it. The scene is a symptom of passions which quite overshadow it, and which we have for long been observing: it does not create passions; it does not introduce a new emotional turn of situation; there is no use made of such external, introduced elements as Anna Karenina's scene with her husband, when he is ill, which suddenly, as it were, "arrives," to make her relationship with Vronsky seem superficial. The scene does, in a word, end a phase, rather than begin a new one: it is like a nervous breakdown which we have so long watched developing, that the symptoms, when they actually emerge, are a relief from protracted neurosis.

The advantage of the Jamesian method is that the drama has organic growth, and is able to proceed unaided by the introduction of new, accidental material from a world developing outside and independently of the world created in the novel. The danger of this method is to make the novel too self-sufficient, and, while it belongs to a "realistic" tradition (it purports to describe "real" characters and real "events": and it is not stylized), to ignore what is generally recognized as reality.

Nevertheless, James's approach is not untrue to life: it is not even less "realistic" than that of the novel based on a dramatic tradition. For the grand *scène passionnelle* is a symptom, but not the root of passion. Passionate activity is intellectual activity. His realization of this is James's great contribution to the novel. The effect of passion is not a momentary display, but a stimulus to thought, which is at once dazzling and intricate. For example, if I am angry about something, the scene in whch I display my anger is only a symptom, or at best a cure, of anger. My anger is a continual train of thought expressing itself in many visions, sounds and colors.

I have tried, therefore, to show not only that James's artistic method was justified, but also that his account of our society makes, in effect, an indictment as fierce as that of Baudelaire: or, indeed, of a class-conscious Marxist writer. Therefore, if I am still faced with the problem of his unreadability, of some obstacle that prevents his interest in life ever meeting that of the general reader, it seems possible that the cause of this difficulty is something much more fundamental than has been expected.

The real difficulty in Henry James lies in his inescapable individualism. He never found in life a subject that completely dragged him out of himself. It will be remembered that at the opening of *The Golden Bowl* Maggie Verver and her father are continually faced with their own selfishness. Their problem is, as I have said, to invent some new marriage, by which they can divorce themselves from their own inner world of a marriage between father and daughter, and create a new synthesis, a marriage of the inner with the external world. That was James's own problem. The most objective of writers, his values are yet entirely personal, in the sense that they are wholly acceptable only to a person whose isolation of experience is identified with his own. For example, his attitude to love is not, as has been said, that of a prude, nor yet that of a lover, certainly not of a Donne! It is that of a person who, profoundly with his whole being, after overcoming great inhibition, has accepted the *idea* of people loving. No description of people loving is more moving than his account of Charlotte and Amerigo falling, as it were, into each other's arms. The situation, where the husband of the daughter vows with the wife of the father that they will always protect the father and daughter—and then they break down—has the stain of evil in it which one finds in the Elizabethans. It might be the Duchess of Malfi claiming Antonio. But this is how James describes it . . . :

> "It's sacred," she breathed back to him. They vowed it, gave it out and took it in, drawn, by their intensity, more closely together. Then of a sudden, through this tightened circle, as at the issue of a narrow strait into the sea beyond, everything broke up, broke down, gave way, melted and mingled. Their lips sought their lips, their pressure their response and their response their pressure; with a violence that had sighed itself the next moment to the longest and deepest of stillnesses they passionately sealed their pledge.

Here is Webster:

DUCH.: . . . Go, go brag
You have left me heartless; mine is in your bosom:
I hope 'twill multiply love there. You do tremble:
Make not your heart so dead a piece of flesh,
To fear more than to love me. Sir, be confident:
What is't distracts you? This is flesh and blood, sir;
'Tis not the figure cut in alabaster
Kneels at my husband's tomb. Awake, awake, man!

I do here put off all vain ceremony,
And only do appear to you a young widow
That claims you for her husband, and, like a widow,
I use but half a blush in't.

ANT.: Truth speak for me;
I will remain the constant sanctuary
Of your good name.

DUCH.: I thank you, gentle love:
And 'cause you shall not come to me in debt,
Being now my steward, here upon your lips
I sign your *Quietus est*. This you should have begged now:
I have seen children oft eat sweetmeats thus,
As fearful to devour them too soon.

Comparing these two passages, one sees in a striking way the effect of Puritan culture, in the repressed and yet desperately courageous imagery of James.

James, after a lifetime of deep human understanding, has arrived at a stage where in suffering and pity he could accept the fact of physical love. The incident that to most people would seem most simple, most common, and yet most peculiar and isolated, is to him universalized as part of the whole cosmos. He cannot make lovers kiss without seeming to cry out, "I accept this with pity and understanding, just as I accept with my mind everything that is life—and hence the proper subject for Art." So the lips that meet are not Charlotte's and the prince's, they are the lips of all lovers; and yet they are no lips and no lovers, they are the symbols of James's spiritual acceptance. Whereas Webster in his great play is suddenly able to clinch the reality and the isolation of his lovers by making them speak poetry in the language of prose (he knows that, given their moment of ecstasy, their language cannot fail to be poetry, so the less poetic it is, the better), James is borne away on a flood of poetry which almost drowns his lovers.

His approach to love, his approach to life, his approach to the obvious, is by way of a North-West Passage. The reader never escapes for a moment from the long journey James has made, and on which he is required to accompany him. He cannot watch someone sign a cheque, or give a kiss, or hail a four-wheeler, without being drowned by waves, or smothered in flowers of James's peculiar mental voyage.

The fact is, that whilst the subject of James's book is his morality, and the working out of that morality of love and intelligence in his characters, this morality is fogged and confused by the fact that a very great deal of his work is about nothing except that he is a New Englander who has spent his life trying to reconcile a Puritan New England code of morals with his idea of the European tradition. This obstructive element is so obvious in his work that he himself was unconscious of it and tried to exploit it by a number of devices. What I wish especially to be noticed is that it affected his actual choice of subjects: on that account he devised the "International Situation," as he called it, and sent his Americans to Europe, and his Europeans to America. So that what he actually wrote about was decided by a peculiarity of his situation, which it is absurd to expect his reader to share: all his reader can do is imaginatively to enter into it. The privilege the reader is offered is to become Henry James, a highly sensitive, cultured man, with extremely isolated spiritual experiences. Of course, as I have tried to show, there is much more to James than that; but it is this extreme individualism of James in his whole attitude to experience that makes him difficult to read. When one reads James, one is, the whole time, unconsciously compelled to identify one's situation in the universe with his own. One has to accept what one might call the secondary political consequences of his ethic: the necessity of having a large income in order to lead a morally significant life; rules of conduct which make the whole style of conversation become based on gossip and tittle-tattle, and which yet prevent people from saying the important things even about their relationships with one another. All these superficialities, which so irritate readers of James, are really part of the ritual of his belief in individualism.

I have tried to show how these whims of James's are really linked up with very important convictions which often fundamentally contradict all that lies on the surface. But when we are dealing with a private creed, we need not be surprised if we find contradictions and obscurities . . . there are enough contradictions in our public beliefs. No one is in the least surprised when an ex-Major, who regards war as the embrace of a lover, writes, "The war gave more life, not less. Yes, life, in spite of all the lives we lost. I feel it, as I stand in the loveliest of all the gardens of our unforgotten dead, looking down on the still waters of the moat at Ypres." Followed by, "But another war? not that! The idea brings with it a feeling of horror and despair."[1] James was living in a society whose life is made tolerable by accepting, with an air of joyful mystery, such fundamental contradictions. His own attitude to the war was almost as ambiguous.

James repeatedly insisted, in all sincerity, that he had no political opinion. But actually his writings are full of negative opinion, expressed in his admiration of a system that keeps the kind of society, which he writes about, alive. The contradiction in James is the contradiction that has affected the writing of most writers of the late nineteenth, and of this century. On the one hand, he is a rebel against the political and economic corruption of his time: he appears as the champion of art against the philistinism of parliamentary ambition. On the other hand, because he is an individualist, because he has worked out in his books his own private system of ethics, which makes it possible for the individual to live aesthetically and morally, in spite of the world around him, he becomes finally a snob, and a supporter of the system, which still makes this existence possible *in spite* of circumstances. To say this is not to say that he lost his integrity: it is, rather, to say that he found it. He saw through the political and social life of his time, but he cherished the privilege which enabled him to see through it.

The life which James wrote about is now as dead as mutton, and in a sense it never was alive. The morality, which is the true subject his novels illustrate, requires for his purpose an ordered society, an aristocracy, and statesman-like figures commanding positions of power. Remaining true to the realistic tradition of the European novel, he described an Anglo-Saxon society, but exercised all his remarkable power of fantasy (perhaps fantasy is his most peculiar gift) in creating a grand worldly scene in which the wealth of upstarts is as expressive as the wealth of a Renaissance prince. In his novels the royalties and aristocrats are so surrounded by an atmosphere of snobbery, that the snobbery creates an effect of anachronism: the royalties are royal and the aristocrats are real. In fact, James invented the position of his characters: or rather,

[1] F. Yeats-Brown, *The Dogs of War.*

by a most ingenious turn of his art, he made his characters invent themselves: for is not Maggie Verver inventing herself all the while as "the princess"? And James's role is simply never on any account to betray that she is ridiculous in doing so.

James ought to have written about kings and queens: but, of course, kings and queens are not available to the modern artist, and are far too available to the newspapers: so he therefore had to enhance unknown well-bred scoundrels, like Amerigo, with a legend of social snobbery. He ought to have written about popes, cardinals, and politicians who exert a great deal of worldly power; but today there are no holders of power that is a recognized and established value, in the sense that Richelieu had power; the power-mongers keep well behind the scenes: he therefore had to write about monsters who have accumulated mountains of corrupt wealth. Nice monsters, like Mr. Verver, or very bad monsters, like the two old men in *The Ivory Tower*. Lastly, he should have been free to write about lovers; but unfortunately in the world he was describing there was no element of innocence. The only way in which he could free his lovers from the disgrace of "money-making" was to make them heirs, and to make them heirs was to damn them, as we see both in *The Wings of the Dove* and, more savagely, in *The Ivory Tower*.

James tried, of course, to write political novels, but the political subject tended to political satire, in *The Princess Casamassima* and *The Tragic Muse*. In order to express moral values he had to invent human values.

In the same way as James is a political-moral artist without a realistic subject drawn from contemporary life to correspond with his ultimate, ethical subject, so Joyce seems to me a religious artist. After his gigantic effort to impose epic values on the modern world, accepted even at its most sordid, he had been compelled not only to invent subjective symbols, but to invent a new language. The same kind of subjectivism, though in an elaborately disguised form, exists in Wyndham Lewis's most ambitious novel, *The Apes of God*.

The key to the subjectivism of all these writers is an intense dissatisfaction with modern political institutions.

# The Private Universe

*by Graham Greene*

The technical qualities of Henry James's novels have been so often and so satisfactorily explored, notably by Mr. Percy Lubbock, that perhaps I may be forgiven for ignoring James as the fully conscious craftsman in order to try to track the instinctive, the poetic writer back to the source of his fantasies. In all writers there occurs a moment of crystallization when the dominant theme is plainly expressed, when the private universe becomes visible even to the least sensitive reader. Such a crystallization is Hardy's often-quoted phrase: "The President of the Immortals . . . had ended his sport with Tess," or that passage in his preface to *Jude the Obscure,* when he writes of "the fret and fever, derision and disaster, that may press in the wake of the strongest passion known to humanity." It is less easy to find such a crystallization in the works of James, whose chief aim was always to dramatize, who was more than usually careful to exclude the personal statement, but I think we may take the sentence in the scenario of *The Ivory Tower,* in which James speaks of "the black and merciless things that are behind great possessions" as an expression of the ruling fantasy which drove him to write: a sense of evil religious in its intensity.

"Art itself," Conrad wrote, "may be defined as a single-minded attempt to render the highest kind of justice to the visible universe," and no definition in his own prefaces better describes the object Henry James so passionately pursued, if the word visible

"The Private Universe." (Originally entitled "Henry James: The Private Universe.") From *The English Novelists,* edited by Derek Verschoyle (London: Chatto & Windus, 1936), reprinted in *The Lost Childhood and Other Essays* (New York: The Viking Press, Inc., 1951) by Graham Greene, pp. 21-30. Copyright 1951 by Graham Greene. Reprinted by permission of The Viking Press, Inc., and Laurence Pollinger, Ltd.

does not exclude the private vision. If there are times when we feel, in *The Sacred Fount,* even in the exquisite *Golden Bowl,* that the judge is taking too much into consideration, that he could have passed his sentence on less evidence, we have always to admit as the long record of human corruption unrolls that he has never allowed us to lose sight of the main case; and because his mind is bent on rendering even evil "the highest kind of justice," the symmetry of his thought lends the whole body of his work the importance of a system.

No writer has left a series of novels more of one moral piece. The differences between James's first works and his last are only differences of art as Conrad defined it. In his early work perhaps he rendered a little less than the highest kind of justice; the progress from *The American* to *The Golden Bowl* is a progress from a rather crude and inexperienced symbolization of truth to truth itself: a progress from evil represented rather obviously in terms of murder to evil *in propria persona,* walking down Bond Street, charming, cultured, sensitive—evil to be distinguished from good chiefly in the complete egotism of its outlook. They are complete anarchists, these late Jamesian characters, they form the immoral background to that extraordinary period of haphazard violence which anticipated the First World War: the attempt on Greenwich Observatory, the siege of Sidney Street. They lent the tone which made possible the cruder manifestations presented by Conrad in *The Secret Agent.* Merton Densher, who planned to marry the dying Milly Theale for her money, plotting with his mistress who was her best friend; Prince Amerigo, who betrayed his wife with her friend, her father's wife; Horton, who swindled his friend Gray of his money: the last twist (it is always the friend, the intimate who betrays) is given to these studies of moral corruption. They represent an attitude which had been James's from very far back; they are not the slow painful fruit of experience. The attitude never varied from the time of *The American* onwards. Mme de Bellegarde, who murdered her husband and sold her daughter, is only the first crude presentation of a woman gradually subtilized, by way of Mme Merle in *The Portrait of a Lady,* into the incomparable figures of evil, Kate Croy and Charlotte Stant.

This point is of importance. James has been too often regarded as a novelist of superficial experience, as a painter of social types, who was cut off by exile from the deepest roots of experience (as if there were something superior in the Sussex or Shropshire of the localized talent to James's international scene). But James was not in that sense an exile; he could have dispensed with the international scene as easily as he dispensed with all the world of Wall Street finance. For the roots were not in Venice, Paris, London; they were in himself. Densher, the Prince, just as much as the red-haired valet Quint and the adulterous governess, were rooted in his own character. They were there when he wrote *The American* in 1876; all he needed afterwards to perfect his work to his own impeccable standard was technical subtlety and that other subtlety which comes from superficial observation, the ability to construct convincing masks for his own personality.

I do not use superficial in any disparaging sense. If his practice pieces, from *The Europeans* to *The Tragic Muse,* didn't engage his full powers, and were certainly not the vehicle for his most urgent fantasies, they were examples of sharp observation, the fruits of a direct objective experience, unsurpassed in their kind. He never again proved himself capable of drawing a portrait so directly, with such command of relevant detail. We know Charlotte Stant, of course, more thoroughly than we know Miss Birdseye in *The Bostonians,* but she emerges gradually through that long book, we don't "see" her with the immediacy that we see Miss Birdseye:

> She was a little old lady, with an enormous head; that was the first thing Ransom noticed—the vast, fair, protuberant, candid, ungarnished brow, surmounting a pair of weak, kind, tired-looking eyes. . . . The long practice of philanthropy had not given accent to her features; it had rubbed out their transitions, their meanings. . . . In her large countenance her dim little smile scarcely showed. It was a mere sketch of a smile, a kind of instalment, or payment on account; it seemed to say that she would smile more if she had time, but that you could see, without this, that she was gentle and easy to beguile. . . . She looked as if she had spent her life on platforms, in audiences, in conventions, in phalansteries, in *séances;* in her faded face there was a kind of reflection of ugly lecture-lamps.

No writer's apprentice work contains so wide and brilliant a range of portraits from this very early Miss Birdseye to Mrs. Brookenham in *The Awkward Age:*

> Mrs. Brookenham was, in her forty-first year, still charmingly pretty, and the nearest approach she made at this moment to meeting her son's description of her was by looking beautifully desperate. She had about her the pure light of youth—would always have it; her head, her figure, her flexibility, her flickering colour, her lovely silly eyes, her natural quavering tone, all played together towards this effect by some trick that had never yet been exposed. It was at the same time remarkable that—at least in the bosom of her family—she rarely wore an appearance of gaiety less qualified than at the present juncture; she suggested for the most part the luxury, the novelty of woe, the excitement of strange sorrows and the cultivation of fine indifferences. This was her special sign—an innocence dimly tragic. It gave immense effect to her other resources.

*The Awkward Age* stands formidably between the two halves of James's achievement. It marks his decision to develop finally from *The American* rather than from *The Europeans.* It is the surrender of experience to fantasy. He hadn't found his method, but he had definitely found his theme. One may regret, in some moods, that his more superficial books had so few successors (English literature has too little that is light, lucid and witty), but one cannot be surprised that he discarded many of them from the collected edition while retaining so crude a fiction as *The American,* discarded even the delicate, feline *Washington Square,* perhaps the only novel in which a man has successfully invaded the feminine field and produced work comparable to Jane Austen's.

How could he have done otherwise if he was to be faithful to his deeper personal fantasy? He wrote of "poor Flaubert" that

> he stopped too short. He hovered for ever at the public door, in the outer court, the splendour of which very properly beguiled him, and in which he seems still to stand as upright as a sentinel and as shapely as a statue. But that immobility and even that erectness were paid too dear. The shining arms were meant to carry further, the outer doors were meant to open. He should at least have listened at the chamber of the soul. This would have floated him on a deeper tide; above all it would have calmed his nerves.

His early novels, except *The American,* certainly belonged to the outer court. They had served their purpose, he had improved his masks, he was never to be more witty; but when he emerged from them again to take up his main study of corruption in *The Wings of the Dove* he had amazingly advanced: instead of murder, the more agonizing mental violence; instead of Mme de Bellegarde, Kate Croy; instead of the melodramatic heroine Mme de Cintré, the deeply felt, subjective study of Milly Theale.

For to render the highest justice to corruption you must retain your innocence: you have to be conscious all the time within yourself of treachery to something valuable. If Peter Quint is to be rooted in you, so must the child his ghost corrupts; if Osmond, Isabel Archer too. These centers of innocence, these objects of treachery, are nearly always women: the lovely daring Isabel Archer, who goes out in her high-handed wealthy way to meet life and falls to Osmond; Nanda, the young girl "coming out," who is hemmed in by a vicious social set; Milly Theale, sick to death just at the time when life has most to offer, surrendering to Merton Densher and Kate Croy (apart from Quint and the Governess the most driven and "damned" of all James's character); Maggie Verver, the unsophisticated "good" young American who encounters her particular corruption in the Prince and Charlotte Stant; the child Maisie tossed about among grown-up adulteries. These are the points of purity in the dark picture.

The attitude of mind which dictated these situations was a permanent one. Henry James had a marvelous facility for covering up his tracks (can we be blamed if we assume he had a reason?). In his magnificent prefaces he describes the geneses of his stories, where they were written, the method he adopted, the problems he faced: he seems, like the conjurer with rolled sleeves, to show everything. But you have to go further back than the anecdote at the dinner table to trace the origin of such urgent fantasies. In this exploration his prefaces, even his autobiographies, offer very little help. Certainly they give his model for goodness; he is less careful to obliterate *that* trail back into youth (if one can speak of care in connection with a design which was probably only half-conscious if it was conscious at all). His cousin, Mary Temple, was the model, a model in her deadly sickness and her high courage, above all in her hungry grip on life, for Milly Theale in particular.

> She had [James wrote of her] beyond any equally young creature I have known a sense for verity of character and play of life in others, for their acting out of their force or their weakness, whatever either might be, at no matter what cost to herself. . . . Life claimed her and used her and beset her—made her range in her groping, her naturally immature and unlighted way from end to end of the scale. . . . She was absolutely afraid of nothing she might come to by living with enough sincerity and enough wonder; and I think it is because one was to see her launched on that adventure in such bedimmed, such almost tragically compromised conditions that one is caught by her title to the heroic and pathetic mark.

Mary Temple then, whatever mark she wore, was always the point of purity, but again one must seek further if one is to trace the source of James's passionate distrust in human nature, his sense of evil. Mary Temple was experience, but that other sense, one feels, was born in him, was his inheritance.

It cannot but seem odd how little in his volumes of reminiscence, *A Small Boy and Others* and *Notes of a Son and Brother,* Henry James really touches the subject of his family. His style is at its most complex: the beauty of the books is very like the beauty of Turner's later pictures: they are all air and light: you have to look a long while into their glow before you discern the most tenuous outline of their subjects. Certainly of the two main figures, Henry James, Senior, and William James, you learn nothing of what must have been to them of painful importance: their sense of daemonic possession.

James was to draw the figure of Peter Quint with his little red whiskers and his white damned face, he was to show Densher and Kate writhing in their hopeless infernal sundering success; evil was overwhelmingly part of his visible universe; but the sense (we get no indication of it in his reminiscences) was a family sense. He shared it with his father and brother and sister. One may find the dark source of his deepest fantasy concealed in a family life which for sensitive boys must have been almost ideally free from compulsions, a tolerant cultured life led between Concord and Geneva. For nearly two years his father was intermittently attacked by a sense of "perfectly insane and abject terror" (his own words); a damned shape seemed to squat beside him raying out "a fetid influence." Henry James's sister, Alice, was a prey to suicidal tendencies, and William James suffered in much the same way as his father.

> I went one evening into a dressing-room in the twilight to procure some article that was there; when suddenly there fell upon me without any warning, just as if it came out of the darkness, a horrible fear of my own existence. Simultaneously there arose in my mind the image of an epileptic patient whom I had seen in the asylum, a black-haired youth with greenish skin, entirely idiotic, who used to sit all day on one of the benches, or rather shelves against the wall, with his knees drawn up against his chin, and the coarse grey undershirt, which was his only garment, drawn over them enclosing his entire figure. . . . This image and my fear entered into a species of combination with each other. *That shape am I,* I felt potentially. Nothing that I possess can defend me against that fate, if the hour for it should strike for me as it struck for him. There was such a horror of him, and such a perception of my own merely momentary discrepancy from him, that it was as if something hitherto solid within my breast gave way entirely, and I became a mass of quivering fear. After this the universe was changed for me altogether. I awoke morning after morning with a horrible dread at the pit of my stomach, and with a sense of the insecurity of life, that I never knew before. . . . It gradually faded, but for months I was unable to go out into the dark alone.

This epileptic idiot, this urge toward death, the damned shape, are a more important background to Henry James's novels than Grosvenor House and late Victorian society. It is true that the moral anarchy of the age gave him his material, but he would not have treated it with such intensity if it had not corresponded with his private fantasy. They were materialists, his characters, but you cannot read far in Henry James's novels without realizing that their creator was not a materialist. If ever a man's imagination was clouded by the Pit, it was James's. When he touches this nerve, the fear of spiritual evil, he treats the reader with less than his usual frankness: "a fairy-tale pure and simple," something seasonable for Christmas, is a disingenuous description of *The Turn of the Screw*. One cannot avoid a conviction that here he touched and recoiled from an important inhibition.

It was just because the visible universe which he was so careful to treat with the highest kind of justice was determined for him at an early age that his family background is of such interest. There are two other odd gaps in his autobiographies; his two brothers, Wilky and Bob, play in them an infinitesimal part. To Miss Burr, the editor of Alice James's Journal, we owe most of our knowledge of these almost commonplace, almost low-brow members of a family intellectual even to excess. To Wilky "the act of reading was inhuman and repugnant"; he wrote from his brigade, "Tell Harry that I am waiting anxiously for his 'next.' I can find a large sale for any blood-and-thunder tale among the darks." From his brigade: that was the point. It was the two failures, Wilky and Bob, who at eighteen and seventeen represented the family on the battlefields of the Civil War. William's eyesight was always bad, and Henry escaped because of an accident, the exact nature of which has always remained a mystery. One is glad, of course, that he escaped the obvious effects of war: Wilky was ruined physically, Bob nervously; both drifted in the manner of wartime heroes from farming in Florida to petty business careers in Milwaukee; and it is not improbable that the presence of these ruined heroes helped to keep Henry James out of America.

Is it possible that through Wilky and Bob we can trace the source of James's main fantasy, the idea of treachery which was always attached to his sense of evil? James had not, so far as we know, been betrayed, like Monteith, like Gray, like Milly Theale and Maggie Verver and Isabel Archer, by his best friend, and it would have taken surely a very deep betrayal to explain an impulse which dictated *The American* in 1876 and *The Golden Bowl* in 1905, which attached itself to the family sense of supernatural evil and produced his great gallery of the damned. It takes some form of self-betrayal to dip so deep, and one need not go, like some of his modern critics, to a "castration complex" to find the reason. There are psychological clues which point to James having evaded military service with insufficient excuse. A civil war is not a continental squabble; its motives are usually deeper, represent less superficial beliefs on the part of the ordinary combatant, and the James family at Concord were at the very spot where the motives of the North sounded at their noblest. His accident has an air of mystery about it (that is why some of his critics have imagined a literal castration), and one needs some explanation of his almost hysterical participation in the Great War on the side of a civilization about which he had no illusions, over whose corruption he had swapped amusing anecdotes with Alice. It will be remembered that in his magnificent study of treachery, *A Round of Visits,* Monteith's betrayer, like all the others, was a very near friend. "To live thus with his unremoved, undestroyed, engaging, treacherous face, had been, as our traveller desired, to live with all of the felt pang." His unremoved face, the felt pang: it is not hard to believe that James suffered from a long subconscious uneasiness about a personal failure.

This, then, was his visible universe: visible indeed if it faced him daily in his glass: the treachery of friends, the meanest kind of lies, "the black and merciless things," as he wrote in the scenario of *The Ivory Tower,* "that are behind great possessions." But it is perhaps the measure of his greatness, of the wideness and justice of his view, that critics of an older generation, Mr. Desmond MacCarthy among them, have seen him primarily as a friendly, rather covetous follower of the "best" society. The sense of evil never obsessed him, as it obsessed Dostoievsky; he never ceased to be primarily an artist, unlike those driven geniuses, Lawrence and Tolstoy, and he could always throw off from the superfluity of his talent such exquisite amiable fragments as "Daisy Miller" and "The Pension Beaurepas": satire so gentle, even while so witty, that it has the quality of nostalgia, a looking back toward a way of life simple and unreflecting, with a kind of innocence even in its greed. "Common she might be," he wrote of Daisy Miller, "yet what provision was made by that epithet for her queer little native grace." It is in these diversions, these lovely little marginalia, that the Marxist critic, just as much as Mr. MacCarthy, finds his material. He was a social critic only when he was not a religious one. No writer was more conscious that he was at the end of a period, at the end of the society he knew. It was a revolution he quite explicitly foresaw; he spoke of

> the class, as I seemed to see it, that had had the longest and happiest innings in history . . . and for whom the future wasn't going to be, by most signs, anything like so bland and benedictory as the past. . . . I cannot say how vivid I felt the drama so preparing might become —that of the lapse of immemorial protection, that of the finally complete exposure of the immemorially protected.

But the Marxists, just as much as the older critics, are dwelling on the marginalia. Wealth may have been almost invariably connected with the treacheries he described, but so was passion. When he was floating on his fullest tide, "listening" as he put it, "at the chamber of the soul," the evil of capitalist society is an altogether inadequate explanation of his theme. It was not the desire for money alone which united Densher and Kate, and the author of *The Spoils of Poynton* would no more have condemned passion than the author of *The Ambassadors* would have condemned private wealth. His lot and his experience happened to lie among the great possessions, but "the black and merciless things" were no more intrinsically part of a capitalist than of a socialist system: they belonged to human nature. They amounted really to this: an egotism so complete that you could believe that something inhuman, supernatural, was working there through the poor devils it had chosen.

In *The Jolly Corner* Brydon, the cultured American expatriate, returned to his New York home and found it haunted. He hunted the ghost down. It was afraid of him (the origin of that twist is known to us. In *A Small Boy* James has described the childish dream he built his story on). He drove it to bay in its evening dress under the skylight in the hall, discovered in the "evil, odious, blatant, vulgar" features the reflection of himself. This was what he would have been if he had stayed and joined the Wall Street racket and prospered. It is easy to take the mere social criticism implied, but I have yet to find socialist or conservative who can feel any pity for the evil *he* denounces, and the final beauty of James's stories lies in their pity: "The poetry is in the pity." His egotists, poor souls, are as pitiable as Lucifer. The woman Brydon loved had also seen the ghost; he had not appeared less blatant, less vulgar to her with his ruined sight and maimed hand and million a year, but the emotion she chiefly felt was pity.

> "He has been unhappy, he has been ravaged," she said.
>
> "And haven't I been unhappy? Am not I—you've only to look at me!—ravaged?"
>
> "Ah, I don't say I like him *better,*" she granted after a thought. "But he's grim, he's worn—and things have happened to him. He doesn't make shift, for sight, with your charming monocle."

James wasn't a prophet, he hadn't a didactic purpose; he wished only to render the highest kind of justice, and you cannot render the highest kind of justice if you hate. He was a realist: he had to show the triumphs of egotism; he was a realist: he had to show that a damned soul has its chains. Milly Theale, Maggie Verver, these "good" people had their escapes, they were lucky in that they loved, could sacrifice themselves like Wilky and Bob, they were never quite alone on the bench of desolation. But the egotists had no escape, there was no tenderness in their passion and their pursuit of money was often no more than an interest, a hobby: they were, inescapably, themselves. Kate and Merton Densher get the money for which they'd schemed; they don't get each other. Charlotte Stant and the Prince satisfy their passion at the expense of a lifetime of separation.

This is not "poetic justice"; it was not as a moralist that James designed his stories, but as a realist. His family background, his personal failure, determined his view of the visible universe when he first began to write, and there was nothing in the society of his time to make him reconsider his view. He had always been strictly just to the truth as he saw it, and all that his deepening experience had done for him was to alter a murder to an adultery, but while in *The American* he had not pitied the murderer, in *The Golden Bowl* he had certainly learned to pity the adulterers. There was no victory for human beings, that was his conclusion; you were punished in your own way, whether you were of God's or the Devil's party. James believed in the supernatural, but he saw evil as an equal force with good. Humanity was cannon fodder in a war too balanced ever to be concluded. If he had been guilty himself of the supreme egotism of preserving his own existence, he left the material, in his profound unsparing analysis, for rendering even egotism the highest kind of justice, of giving the devil his due.

> It brought Spencer Brydon to his feet. "You 'like' that horror—?"
> "I *could* have liked him. And to me," she said, "he was no horror, I had accepted him."

"I had accepted him." James, who had never taken a great interest in his father's Swedenborgianism, had gathered enough to strengthen his own older more traditional heresy. For his father believed, in his own words, that "the evil or hellish element in our nature, even when out of divine order . . . is yet not only no less vigorous than the latter, but on the contrary much more vigorous, sagacious and productive of eminent earthly uses" (so one might describe the acquisition of Milly Theale's money). The difference, of course, was greater than the resemblance. The son was not an optimist, he didn't share his father's hopes of the hellish element, he only pitied those who were immersed in it; and it is in the final justice of his pity, the completeness of an analysis which enabled him to pity the most shabby, the most corrupt, of his human actors, that he ranks with the greatest of creative writers. He is as solitary in the history of the novel as Shakespeare in the history of poetry.

# Symbolic Imagery

*by Austin Warren*

The general occasions of the "last period" are tolerably clear, if scarcely of the same order of being. There is, first, the gradual loss of the larger audience reached by "Daisy Miller" and the novels of Howells; then, the judgment that country-house week ends and the "season" in London had already provided saturation; then, the shift, in compositional method, from writing to dictation; then, the impetus of admiration from sympathetic younger writers and the allied, induced, partial participation in the new literary movement of the Nineties, the "aesthetic" movement associated with the names of Pater, Wilde, Harland, the *Yellow Book,* and—by extension—of Stevenson, Conrad, Crane, Ford Madox Ford; then, the just completed period of writing for the theater, which produced not only *Guy Domville* but also a conception of the novel as drama; last, the influence, through Maeterlinck and, especially, the later Ibsen, of *symbolisme,* and the return thereby to Hawthorne and a deeper psychology.

The retirement to Rye, which occurred in 1897 when James was fifty-four, distinguished between his life of experience and his life from "past accumulations" (as he once called it). His peregrinations over, he set himself, masterwise, to producing a world compact of all that he had been able, coherently, to think and feel.

Then the process of dictation, beginning with *The Spoils of Poynton,* had its psychological and stylistic consequences. A timid, slow-speaking, stammering boy, Henry had rarely been able to

"Symbolic Imagery." (Originally entitled "Henry James: Symbolic Imagery in the Later Novels.") From *Rage for Order* by Austin Warren, pp. 142-161. Copyright © 1959 by Austin Warren. Reprinted by permission of the University of Michigan Press.

make himself heard at the parental breakfast table. Dictation offered dictatorship: his own voice, uninterrupted by those of more rapid speakers, enabled him to have his oral say in a style which is nearer to his father's than to William's, but slower than his father's. Henry's later manner is an allegro slowed down to a largo, the conversational in apotheosis. "Literary" as, all sprinkled with its commas of parenthesis, it looks on paper, it is an oral style; and, verifiably, it becomes clear, almost luminous, if recommitted to the voice.

This oral tone was certainly abetted by James's steady turn toward the drama. Rather early, Henry wrote his brother of having mastered the dramatic technique of those makers of the "well-made play," Augier and Sardou. He was, of course, an admirer of the Comédie Française and so, we may think, of Molière and Racine. To the French classical drama, as well as to Sardou, I should attribute his increasing use, in his later work, of structure fairly to be called neoclassical, geometrical: wing matching wing, and pilaster corresponding to pilaster, in designs sometimes monstrous in their regularity.

The drama of the Nineties, Maeterlinck and, especially, Ibsen, had its effect on the later novels in which, though the author proudly renounces his right of omniscience, he returns triumphantly in the mode of tonality, figuration, almost color scheme. The relation between Kate and Milly, in *The Wings of the Dove,* becomes, at one point, the "likeness of some dim scene in a Maeterlinck play; we have positively the image, in the delicate dusk, of the figures so associated and yet so opposed, so mutually watchful: that of the angular pale princess, ostrich-plumed, black-robed—hung about with amulets, reminders, relics—mainly seated, mainly still; and that of the upright, restless, slow-circling lady of her court who exchanges with her, across the black water streaked with evening gleams, fitful questions and answers." There is no question of wholesale admiration. It is the slightly comic because immensely refined and "cultured" Mrs. Susan Shepherd Stringham who "admires" Maeterlinck and Pater; but James respected both and in the former could find warrant for a kind of symbolist drama restricted in characters and in action and unified by tone. Ibsen, whose *Hedda* and *Master Builder* he saw, about whom he wrote (in 1891 and 1893) with regard and discernment, gave him examples of fictional work which were the reverse of improvization. "Wrought with admirable closeness is the whole tissue of relations between the five people whom [in *Hedda*] the author sets in motion and on whose behalf he asks of us so few concessions." "The distinguished thing is the firm hand that weaves the web, the deep and ingenious use made of the material." The more one looks at an Ibsen play, the "more intentions" one sees. There was, in the history of the novel, no precedent so near as Ibsen for the concentration of construction and the symbolism which are characteristic of James in the later novels. The patterns of the two have a general parallel of early romanticism, middle realism, and a late maturity which attempts to create what James attributes to the *Master Builder*—a "mingled reality and symbolism."

In poetic drama—*The Tempest* (on which he wrote an essay), plays of Racine, Maeterlinck, and Ibsen—James came nearest to finding precedents for his later novels. And in these plays are adumbrated the two devices which dominate one's recollection of the later James: close conversation and the metaphor.

Prefacing *The Wings of the Dove,* James differentiated the "picture" from the "drama" as two rival techniques of the novel, a distinction corresponding (I take it) to that between narrative from a "point of view" and direct presentation. After his experiment, in *The Awkward Age,* with the novel as a set of scenes or dialogues uninterrupted by a unifying consciousness, he grew technically aware, and systematically provident, of dialogue in alternation with narrative, a narrative of consciousness and inner soliloquy.

This technical or structural distinction has its epistemological and metaphysical counterpart. James distinguished two modes of knowing: I shall call them dialectic and myth.

One is a cerebral process, pursued by two or more minds, in contrapuntal movement of thesis, antithesis, synthesis. The topic is attacked from without; the speakers circle around it. Like collaborating detectives they piece together their evidence, or like attorneys for the defense and the prosecution they proceed alternately, on rival systems. There are examinations and cross-examinations. There are mutual misunderstandings, false clues, shifts of position.

James liked to read the reports of divorce trials and murders; he was a confessed admirer of Roughead's books. But it is unnecessary to suppose any external incitation to such close, minute, unwearying analysis as James's people carry on. There are people who find a great dinner or ball or simpler occasion quite unsatisfactory unless before, and especially after, the event there is, in collaboration with another critical observer, an exhaustive analysis of the occasion—its persons, the shifts of relation between them, the discovery of unexpected relations, the probable motives of those present, the intent of speeches and interlocutions which baffled immediacy. James was obviously such a person in his talks with Howard Sturgis, A. C. Benson, Edith Wharton, or Paul Bourget.

By the closeness and intensity of the "dialectic" James commits himself: he really believes in the all but supreme importance of personal relationships; and, because they are so important, the proper interpretation of them becomes important. Yet relationships between civilized (deep and subtle) people involve concealments as well as avowals; the more developed, the more affectionally, socially, ethically complicated the people, the more precarious and elaborate their relations, and the more imperative the need of system and persistence in making them out.

Unlike the Socratic dialogues, these progress without the aid of a master-mind to control. Nor are they the dialogues of Racine, though in them we come near to James: Miss Gostrey, Mrs. Assingham, Mrs. Stringham are *ficelles,* are confidants, like Phèdre's nurse, Hippolyte's tutor, and Oreste's friend Pylade. But the characteristic dialogue in Racine pits a passionate protagonist against a professional moderator; we might call it the struggle of judgment against passion. In James's, however, the interlocutors are jointly concerned to understand a situation; their passion goes into their seeing. And the confidants do not merely serve to transform soliloquies into dialogues or to draw out their principals; they confer with one another and with other principals. Mrs. Stringham, for example, serves as "muse" and palace guard and tutor in the "higher and finer things," yet she is also a mind intent and alert for conference with Mrs Lowder and Densher.

The characteristic dialogue of the later novels avoids the long speech—turns, indeed, almost to stichomythia. Even the short speeches are interrupted; and so close is the texture that words and phrases are taken up and returned. Sometimes a figure started by one is developed in turn, after the fashion of *bouts-rimés.* In *The Ivory Tower,* Gray and Horton so collaborate for four pages, as Horton tries to make his friend see the chances to marry, the amorous assailments, which await a rich young American.

The dialogues exhibit the conscious mind working hard and critically scrutinizing all available facts, examining semantically the import of words. This work of intelligence is for James a social act. There is much about ourselves and others which can be got at only in this way; there is a reality which is social, without participation in which we lose our sanity. James seems classical, French, in his whole attitude toward society, intelligence, communication. Unlike Hawthorne's, his people are not tempted by pride to isolate themselves from their fellows; even the shy protagonists are free from pride or inferiority: they reach out their hands to association.

But then there is another kind of truth to be arrived at not socially, intellectually, or analytically but personally, intuitively, imaginatively—through images and symbols. Origins and ends have to be put mythically, as Plato puts them in the *Phaedrus,* the *Gorgias,* the *Republic.* Our reasonings start from an intuition, a total feeling of the nature of the world or the nature of a person; they return constantly to check themselves by that intuition; and it is an intuition upon which, finally, we act. The Jamesian equivalent of myth lies, I think, in the metaphors which, much increasing in *The Wings* over *The Ambassadors,* reach their high richness in *The Bowl* and *The Ivory Tower.*[1]

[1] The three completed masterpieces, *The Ambassadors, The Wings of the Dove,* and *The Golden Bowl,* were written between 1900 and 1904. The order in which these novels were published does not match that of their production: a letter written to Howells in August, 1901, makes clear that *The Ambassadors,* though published a year after *The Wings,* was composed before it; and this discrepancy explains why *The Wings* is in style nearer to *The Bowl.*

Nearly ten years elapsed, years occupied by *The American Scene,* the autobiographical volumes, the revision of the earlier novels, and a return to the writing of plays. Finally, in 1914, when he was seventy, James returned to the novel, first to *The Ivory Tower,* and then, when the war made a contemporary subject unmanageable, to *The Sense of the Past,* a manuscript begun at the period of *The Wings.*

Here we must distinguish two modes of figuration in the later James. The first is the "extended conceit" made by prolonging an image, commonly an image proverbial, trite, conventionally "beautiful." Instances are frequent in novels; in revising the texture of his earlier work for the "New York Edition," James became aware of buried metaphors and resurrected them. Of the following sequence, from *The American* (written in 1877, revised thirty years later), the italicized prelude, anticipating the "sacred fire," was added in 1907: Mrs. Tristram is *"interesting from this sense she gave of her looking for her ideals by a lamp of strange and fitful flame.* She was full—both for good and ill—of beginnings that came to nothing; but she had nevertheless, morally, a spark of the sacred fire." These regalvanized figures, a kind of wit-work, suggest minor "metaphysical" poetry—that of Henry King or Joseph Beaumont.

The second mode is an emblematic perception, a symbolized intuition—in form an original image, sometimes comic, sometimes horrendous, often grotesque. It is these which offer the mythic. The "expressionism" of the later novels makes it difficult to locate, psychologically, all these emblematic perceptions. Some of James's people—his favorite heroines, certainly—are repeatedly asserted to "image" a situation, that is, instinctively to conceive of it in metaphorical terms. But there is perhaps no character—even to Colonel Assingham—who is not occasionally given a metaphor; and I conclude that James thinks of all his characters as having an unconscious, as having a world of instinctive, feeling reactions, reactions which in art must express themselves (even if by intermediation of the novelist) in metaphoric terms.

Recollected images become metaphors. For years James had traveled diligently in France and Italy, written conscientious commentaries on cathedrals, châteaux, and galleries. Now people remind him of art, become indeed works of art. His heroines, almost without exception, are thus translated. The auburn-haired Milly Theale is a Bronzino; Aurora Coyne becomes "an Italian princess of the *cinque cento:* Titian or the grand Veronese might . . . have signed her image." Nan, the modernist and un-British daughter of *The Sense of the Past,* recalls "some mothering Virgin by Van Eyck or Memling." For Maggie there is evoked some slim draped statue from the Vatican, "the smoothed elegant nameless head, the impersonal flit of a creature lost in an alien age." Mme de Vionnet's head could be found on "an old precious medal, some silver coin of the Renaissance," while her daughter is a "faint pastel in an oval frame . . . the portrait of an old-time princess." Some embarrassment prevents similar translation of the heroes into paintings or statues; but the Prince (who is bought, after all, as a work of art and appraised by his father-in-law with the same taste which appraises a Luini) can scarcely be described except out of art history: by way of representing the superior utility and weight of the male, James renders him in architecture. His eyes, for example, prompt the *concetto* of their being "the high windows of a Roman palace, of an historic front by one of the great old designers, thrown open on a feast day to the golden air." And his union to the Ververs, the new "relation" which it establishes, suggests to Adam Verver that "their decent little old-time union, Maggie's and his own, had resembled a good deal some pleasant public square, in the heart of an old city, into which a great Palladian church, say—something with a grand architectural front—had suddenly been dropped."

The obvious errand of these analogies is honorific; they belong to the high and hallowed world of "culture." But in the decorative and the "beautiful," James's taste (like his taste in poetry) was conventional. He had to come to the poetic by misapprehension, one might say, by the way of the unlovely.

Unlike his Prince, who "never saw . . . below a certain social plane," James had looked observantly, in his days of "notation," at zoos and aquariums and circuses; and he remembered the crowded perceptions of "A Small Boy" in a remote America. Having neither children nor wealth, Mrs. Assingham confronted "two great holes to fill, and she described herself as dropping social scraps into them as she had known old ladies, in her early, American time, drop morsels of silk into baskets in which they collected the material for some eventual patchwork quilt." For regression to the "good old," there are the childhood images: Adam Verver, indulging a tiny holiday from responsibility, seems "caught in the act of handling a relic of infancy,—sticking on the head of a broken soldier or trying the lock of a wooden gun." In their continued intimacy after both have other mates, father and daughter were "at times, the dear things, like children playing at visits, playing at 'Mr. Thompson and Mrs. Fane.' "

The chief occasions for "imaging" are perceptions of persons and personal relations. In *The Bowl* and the unfinished novels, the characters are not visualized analytically but felt for us, rendered in terms of the total impression they make. Book I of *The Ivory Tower* is constantly metaphorical, moving into dialectical prose only to chronicle the Bradhams' large, busy tea. Rosanna, her father, the Bradhams, and Cissy Foy, their protégée, appear in poetry. Rosanna's massiveness and heroic stature and indomitability are rendered by the recurrent image of the ship in full sail; her voice rings out like that of Brünnehilde at the opera; her parasol is the "roof of some Burmese palanquin or perhaps even pagoda"; her presence is apprehended by Cissy as that of "some seated idol, a great Buddha perched upon a shrine." [2] Though he owns the literal stage property of a rocking chair on a vacant Newport piazza, Rosanna's father is also "a ruffled hawk, motionless but for his single tremor"; he broods "after the fashion of a philosopher tangled in some maze of metaphysics." When he makes his single shift of gear, from business to his daughter, he passes from his "market" into "some large cool dusky temple, a place where idols others than those of his worship vaguely loomed and gleamed."

The zealous exegete of meanings studies his companions' faces. He sees that Verver's face "resembled a small decent room, clean-swept and unencumbered with furniture, but drawing special advantages . . . from the outlook of a pair of ample and uncurtained windows"; that Davy Bradham's "good worn worldly face, superficially so smooth," had "the sense of it lined and scratched and hacked across much in the manner of the hard ice of a large pond at the end of a long day's skating." Densher notes it "an oddity of Mrs. Lowder's that her face in speech was like a lighted window at night, but that silence immediately drew the curtain."

Our recollection of Mrs. Lowder, James's massive rich British matron, is almost entirely compounded from the imagings of

[2] James's oriental figures are relatively frequent and always to be attended; they habitually betoken the strangeness of that East which is East and hence incommunicable to the West.

Densher, through whose at once admiring and hostile and amused consciousness we chiefly see her. The master metaphor is metallic. We first view her in her cage—all "perpetual satin, twinkling bugles and flashing gems, with a lustre of agate eyes, a sheen of raven hair, a polish of complexion," encased in the hard glittering surface of armor. Later, at the dinner table, managing a conversation, she becomes a steamboat, "steering a course in which she called at subjects as if they were islands in an archipelago," resumes, "with a splash of the screw, her cruise among the islands." Still later she has "something in common, even in repose, with a projectile, of great size, loaded and ready for use."

Mrs. Midmore, briefly presented in *The Sense of the Past,* and Mrs. Newsome, indirectly presented, never seen, belong, by their analogical treatment, to the same category with Mrs. Lowder: they are women as massive as, ultimately, menacing. It is never entirely clear how far Strether understands his feeling toward Mrs. Newsome (or how completely James understands it): Mrs. Newsome is not, like Mrs. Lowder, an obvious case of Philistinism; indeed, she regards herself as an apostle of Culture—of the higher and finer and rarer and newer thought; and James apparently wants to represent Strether as making a sacrifice in renouncing Mrs. Newsome (as well as the more suitable Miss Gostrey). Yet, though the Lady of Woolett represented maternal protection as well as maternal domination, Strether's chief sense, upon losing her, must, like Lewes's upon losing the great Eliot, have been relief.[3] Mrs. Newsome is massive because she has no imagination. She rests, sits, *is*—a fact without resilience. Others, the imaginative, must adjust, accommodate. As he thinks of her, Strether's "eyes might have been fixing some particularly large iceberg in a cool blue northern sea."

If Philistines are to be "imaged" as inflexibly massive, metallic (unimaginative), the children of light owe their erect posture, their equilibrium, to their flexibility. They summon up recollection of ballet dancers, show people, brave ritualists who perform, upon exhibition, feats of persistence and agility: figures proper to Goya, Degas, Toulouse-Lautrec. Assingham watches his wife engaged at her favorite social analysis "much as he had sometimes watched at

[3] I am remembering an anecdote told by Stephen Spender in *The Destructive Element,* one of the best studies of James.

the Aquarium the celebrated lady who, in a slight, though tight, bathing suit, turned somersaults or did tricks in the tank of water which looked so cold and uncomfortable to the non-amphibious." When Maggie, courageously, undertakes a grand dinner at Portland Place, Mrs. Assingham assists "like one of the assistants in the ring at the circus, to keep up the pace of the sleek revolving animal on whose back the lady in short spangled skirts should brilliantly caper and posture." Throughout most of her half of *The Golden Bowl,* Maggie is the "overworked little trapezist girl." The novel rehearses her progress from being a child to being the lady in spangled skirts who can keep her balance while she capers on the back of a horse.

There are other fresh aspects of Maggie to be celebrated—for one, her resourceful Americanism—in contrast to her husband's ancient, aristocratic lineage. By virtue of this difference, Maggie must be expected to do most of the "adjustment": she must act like a "settler or trader in a new country; in the likeness even of some Indian squaw with a papoose on her back and barbarous bead work to sell." But without question there are governing images. As Maggie is the trapezist, so Charlotte, through the corresponding second half of *The Bowl,* is some wild creature, tormented by the gadfly; she is a caged creature which, bending the gilt bars, has escaped to roam; she wears "a long silken halter looped round her beautiful neck."

In the later novels the chief thing, after all, is the structure. The characters exist in relations, and we are unbidden to information about them irrelevant to the fable and the relations. A character might almost be defined as the locus at which a given number of relations join. The Prince, for example, is the total of his relations to Mrs. Assingham, Mr. Verver, Charlotte, and Maggie: though he has to be preliminarily posited as a classic instance of the aristocratic European, James presents that datum as summarily as possible.

One who, like Gray Fielder and his creator, is "critico-analytically interested" in people, gives inevitable attention to defining relationships. His skilled attention delights in the idea of a little set or group (like Mrs. Brook's), capable of developing its own vocabulary of allusions and words; but he specializes in the relation between two. Hawthorne was James's great predecessor in this study, especially in those masterly chapters of *The Scarlet Letter* describing

Chillingworth's sadistic operations on Dimmesdale. Relationships are not static and are never so represented by James; and the change in one relationship affects a corresponding change in another. "Critico-analytical" people do not take fixity of relationship for granted but are constantly attempting to name the new state into which a relationship has entered, the new quality which has emerged. The relations most "imaged" are likely to be those which can least be talked out. Maria Gostrey and Strether do not "image" one another because the relation between them is dialectical; but, since Chad (for all his wonderful renovation) is neither dialectical nor imaginative, Strether has strenuously to use his own intuitive instrument. When Strether first encounters the Paris Version, Chad's "attitude was that of a person who has been gracefully quiet while the messenger at last reaching him has run a mile through the dust." And much later, Strether perceives that Chad "puts out" his excitement or whatever emotion "as he put out his washing. . . . It was quite for Strether himself in short to feel a personal analogy with the laundress bringing home the triumphs of the mangle."

The relation between Merton Densher and Kate Croy, particularly, rewards study, for Densher at least (whom we see more from within than we see Kate) is not only dialectically clever but also passionate. We wonder how he can tolerate Kate's plan or Kate for her plan; but, granting that his conscious mind found it "something so extraordinarily special to Kate that he felt himself shrink from the complications involved in judging it," we discover him, nonetheless, transcending his complicity. He is drawn to her by desire yet repelled as well as fascinated by her calculations. As he looks at her, in the Gallery, the sight plays on his pride of possession, "as a hidden master in a great dim church might play on the grandest organ"; yet this sense of possession is more than matched by apprehension of her calculating power: more than once he said to her, "You keep the key of the cupboard, and I foresee that when we're married you'll dole me out my sugar by lumps."

In *The Sense of the Past,* the most "imaged" relation is between Ralph Pendrel, American introspective, and the blunt, massive, extroverted Perry Midmore, his contrary. When the other Regency and British Midmores are puzzled by the visitor, Perry has the advantage of not being "cultured": he trusts, animal-like, to his instincts, scents the presence of the clever and alien "as some creature of the woods might scent the bait of the trapper. . ."; "like a frightened horse," he "sniffs in the air the nearness of some creature of a sort he has never seen." It is Perry, in turn, who most makes Ralph aware of his general peril, the precariousness of sustaining his role—how he must always use *manner* as a weapon, always "work from *behind* something—something that, look as it would, he must object to Perry's staring at in return as if it were a counterfeit coin or a card from up his sleeve."

The most powerful, most inclusive, vision in this novel sums Ralph's sudden awareness of his 1820 Midmores in their historic, their psychic, distance from him. In a somewhat similar moment of perception, Alice saw her companions as nothing but playing cards. Ralph sees his as waxworks or statues: "an artful, a wonderful trio, some mechanic but consummate imitation of ancient life, staring through the vast plate of a museum." This perception marks the turn from Ralph's desire to live in the past to his countermovement: James's hero, who disappoints his robust lady by his passionate love of the past, his desire to catch "the very tick of the old stopped clocks," is cured of his wish by its fulfillment and at the end returns, happily, to the modern world.

The second half of *The Golden Bowl,* supreme among the later novels for the density and richness of its symbolism, is dominated by Maggie's sense of the relations in which she stands, of which the most stable is with her father, the most precarious and menacing that with her rival, the Dark Lady.

The "imagings"—fear-images, many of them—which crowd the later chapters arise from Maggie's inability to talk out her apprehensions except, and scantily, to Mrs. Assingham. Her relations to her father, the Prince, and Charlotte cannot, by the very nature of her problem and her project, be socially articulated; she must fight soundlessly and in the dark.

When the "little trapezist girl" tries to envisage her plight she often does so in architectural mode. The strangeness which she suddenly stumbles over—Charlotte's affair with the Prince—is an "outlandish pagoda, a structure plated with bright porcelain, colored and figured and adorned at the overhanging eaves with silver bells that tinkled," a pagoda set down in her own familiar, blooming garden. Later, in Book V, she feels the whole horrible situation to constitute the central chamber of a haunted house, "a great overarched and overglazed rotunda where gaiety might reign, but the doors of which opened into sinister circular passages." What Maggie must take in is the possibility of an evil which can appear in a Garden, or in a Home—which is not the villain of a melodrama or the Devil replete with horns. Evil met her, now, "like some bad-faced stranger surprised in one of the thick-carpeted corridors of a house of quiet on a Sunday afternoon." The sense of imprisonment is impossible to avoid, even when it is an enclosure allegedly therapeutic. Shut off from responsibility by the social gifts of her husband and his mistress, Maggie, coming to, finds herself locked up "in the solid chamber of her helplessness as in a bath of benevolence artfully prepared for her. . . . Baths of benevolence were all very well, but at least, unless one was a patient of some sort, a nervous eccentric or a lost child, one usually wasn't so immersed save by one's own request."

These oppressive claustric figures give way, as Maggie turns active, to more agile figures. In Book V, Maggie, feeling like a scapegoat, goes off into the darkness. From the terrace, looking in through the window, she sees her companions glassed, separated off like actors on a stage. Equipped with this perspective, she begins to fight; and even though images of frustration continue, they are intermitted with those of triumph. She overcomes her fear of Charlotte, lies boldly, kisses her with magnanimous treachery, and begins to "image" Charlotte's defeat; psychically hears, issuing from beneath her elegant mask, the "shriek of a soul in pain." Now out of prison, Maggie sees her companions caught: her husband strikes her as being "caged" in his room; and our final view of Charlotte, consigned for shipment to American City, is that of a once living creature now petrified into "some colored and gilded image."

There are *données* of *The Bowl* which are perverse and scarcely to be accepted. Since James cannot really bring himself to "realize" a union at once sexual and "good," the loves of the book are the passion of Charlotte for the Prince and of Maggie for her father. Dialectic, managed by another than James, might usefully have made these presuppositions explicit. But, to the saving of the novel's balance, the violent relation is between two women; and, whatever the pretext or the booty, Maggie becomes aware that evil may meet one garbed as an urbane friend and learns how so to fight evil as to save what she prizes. James's sense of the good is, one might say, temperamentally conditioned; his sense of evil is normal and sound. And the great theme of *The Bowl* is the discovery that evil exists in the forms most disruptive to civilization: in disloyalty and treason.

In spite of the predominance of myth over dialectic in the novel, especially its second half, *The Bowl* does not represent James's escape into a defeatist Unconscious, the collapse of his system of values. Unlike many of his protagonists, Maggie is concerned not only to understand her situation but to will, savingly, and to act, successfully. Her dreams are, ultimately, those not of a patient but of a victor.

The tension in James between the dialectic and the mythic is an epistemological way of naming that rich interplay and reconciliation of impulses which constitutes his great achievement. As a person and as a writer, he matured slowly; he had to confront the long, slow business of synthesizing his impulse to merge and his impulse to withdraw, his shyness and his sociability, his romanticism (his first literary mode) and his realism, his humanism and his mysticism.

If there is the Henry James who speaks of dining out a hundred and seven times in a winter, who is to be "imaged" in the ritual garments—the silk topper, the morning coat, the fawn-colored waistcoat, the gloves folded in hand—there is also the inner James who never leaves the sanctuary, where are the altars of literature, the dead, and the Good.

One must not talk here of appearance and reality, for that is not the relation between this pair. In terms from the characterology (or perhaps hagiography) of James's youth, one can say that the outer self was modeled on Norton or Russell Lowell, while the inner self remained not remote from Emerson—if one may add, from Hawthorne, what James found deficient in Emerson, a "sense of the dark, the foul, the base . . . certain complications in life . . . human perversity." The outer James is an urbane humanist, an intelligent, if precise, defender of convention, usage, social discrimination, and social intelligence; the inner James is an intuitionist, possessed of a deep nonutilitarian, nontraditional faith in goodness for goodness' sake, loyalty to loyalty, *caritas.*

Because James was a "thinker" only on the theory of fiction, he did not schematize, still less adjust, his levels. He reported honestly whatever—material, social, spiritual—he saw. He liked breeding, culture, taste; he perceived that these were the products (even if not the necessary products) of leisure, and leisure, in turn, of money. Yet from youth to age he gave unpleasant pictures of the merely intelligent and cultivated—of the elder Bellegardes, of Osmond and Mme Merle, of Mrs. Gereth, Mrs. Newsome, Mrs. Brookenham. They are all "wonderful" specimens—expensive to produce and engaging to study; but they do not give us our scale. High above the bright and cultivated are the good.

To be sure, he finds it difficult to work out his sum. His "good people" are generally poor, like Fleda Vetch and Strether; when, like Milly Theale and the Ververs, they are rich, it is by fabulous endowment: Adam's alleged power of making money remains unconvincing. By the time he wrote *The Ivory Tower,* James seems to have agreed with the Gospels that the salvation of the rich is precarious. Yet he as clearly believed that salvation—or total salvation—was, in any case, rare. If riches could prevent it, so could envy, brutality, and stupidity, the vices of the poor, or the complacence of "middle-class morality."

This range of standards in James makes him both rewarding and exacting. His irony, which is pervasive, can be most readily detected in his act of praising people for having a virtue or two, virtues on which they plume themselves, when his criterion is a stratified perfection.

The danger of such a philosophy is that, in its awareness, its inclusiveness, it shall turn finally skeptical, or regard uncertainty and complexity as final virtues. This seems, in practice, not to have happened to James: though he probably had his confusions and timidities, he was not awarely proud of them. The general view of him, until fifteen years ago, scaled him down to a caricatured "humanism," that is, to snobbery and Anglophilism—though better evidence can be collected for his disapproval of "high society," for his Americanism and his moralism. He was emphatically not a skeptic or a believer in mutual cancellations. He had a clear hierarchy of values, or, better, a hierarchy of value-series, which he applied with almost equal realism and rigor.

The distinctive, masterly achievement of Henry James in his maturity is a series of "metaphysical" novels in which, working as a poet, he incarnates the interrelations between the conscious and the unconscious, between the social and the subjective.

# The Museum World

*by Adeline Tintner*

> To be at all critically, or as we have been fond of calling it analytically minded . . . is to be subject to the superstition that objects and places, coherently grouped, disposed for human use and addressed to it, must have a sense of their own, a mystic meaning proper to themselves to give out: to give out, that is, to the participant at once so interested and so detached as to be moved to a report of the matter.

In *The American Scene* James gives us the most rewarding clue to the explanation of the many works of art that appear in his fiction. This is the "mystic meaning proper to themselves," and any interpretation of the "things" which ignores these words incurs the danger of not fully explaining them. The defect of Mr. Matthiessen's interesting essay in the 1943 James issue of the *Kenyon Review*[1] stems from his view of the work of art only as an example of compositional strategy. It is quite true that James was concerned with "the possibility of developing multiple points of view" and that he "saw both with and through his eye; and the abundance of his images and scenes gave his art compositional permanence," but the exhibited array of European art had a more complex function in the creation of his fiction. In interpreting the meaning of the works of art as a means of technique, Mr. Matthiessen ignores the "meaning proper to themselves." Viewing them as instruments, he does not see them as ends. Mr. Warren's brilliant essay in the same

"The Museum World," by Adeline Tintner. (Originally entitled "The Spoils of Henry James.") *PMLA,* LXI (1946), 239-251. Reprinted by permission of the author and the Modern Language Association of America.

[1] F. O. Matthiessen, "James and the Plastic Arts," *The Kenyon Review,* v, no. 4 (1943), 533-550.

issue,[2] on the other hand, regards the "recollected images" of the late fiction as iconographic entities rather than as instrumental means. But concentrating on the function of the art object to provide material for the metaphors of the mature work, he excludes from critical control the many references in the early and middle work.

To complete and, in some respects, to modify the picture which Mr. Matthiessen and Mr. Warren have partially indicated, we must proceed from James's own assumption: objects give out a meaning proper to themselves. Tracing this meaning from beginning to end, accepting its variations as they appear in the context of the stories, we conclude that, although at one time it may be strategy for visualizing and, at another, substance for myth, the over-all meaning is that the work of art embodies and incorporates civilization as it was available to James. It acts as protagonist in the total drama. For James's *oeuvre* is the record of an attempt to balance the material aspect of civilization, art—with its spiritual aspect, life. And although he moves from art back again to behavior before he finally adjusts their relationship to each other, there is no moral value ever introduced which cannot be referred to either of them.

The meaning of the works of art in the early fiction is conditioned largely by James's response to the movement of art for art's sake which in America was taken more literally than in Europe. If Pater had abstracted from the experience of the spectator of art a general theory for the validity of the spectator of life, the provincial tendency was to worship the model behind the theory: the picture or the statue of Europe's traditional art. The "aesthetic religion" was embraced most fanatically by those who had turned away from Puritanism, and this may explain why Hawthorne was so reluctant and James so eager to accept the cult. Although *The Marble Faun* created the precedent in American fiction for drama set in an environment of art, Hawthorne continually restricts the action of the setting on his personal conflicts. The limits of the power of art over man are stated when Kenyon says: "I defy any painter to move or elevate me without my own consent and assistance." Its effect as an object of man's creative skill is negligible: as Miriam

[2] Austin Warren, "Myth and Dialectic in the Later Novels," *The Kenyon Review*, v, no. 4 (1943), 551-568.

looks at some portrait busts she thinks "that the outer marble was merely an extraneous environment; the human countenance within its embrace must have existed there since the limestone ledges of Carrara were first made." Art is useful only when it allegorizes the struggle of man's conscience, and Hawthorne's interest in graveyards, which his *Notebooks* rate above picture galleries, shows that a headstone served him better as allegory than did a painting. In James's fiction art is no longer symbolic of the fate of Christian man; it has become a collection of idols in a religion satisfying all human needs. Far from Hilda's realization that art "cannot comfort the heart in affliction; it grows dim when the shadow is upon us," is the belief of the hero of James's "Traveling Companions": "in moments of doubt and depression I find it of excellent use to recall the great picture (Leonardo's *Last Supper*) with all possible distinctness." Rowland Mallett in a personal crisis calms himself by meditating on "the unattainable repose" of Raphael's *Madonna of the Chair*. The complete trust with which James's early characters give themselves to art grew out of the conditions in which James first learned about it. In his autobiographical volumes he recreates the atmosphere of awe:

> Didn't . . . (various artists) . . . more or less haunt our family fireside, and give us also the sense of others, landscapist Cropseys and Coles and Kensetts and bust-producing Iveses and Powerses and Moziers, hovering in an outer circle?

The man who represented "the type—the 'European,' and this gave him an authority for me that it verily took the length of years to undermine"—was the painter, La Farge. The "most hushed of all temples" was the Louvre, and even the houses in the streets of Paris speak as divinities to the young James:

> Yes, small staring *jeune homme,* we are dignity and memory and measure, we are conscience and proportion and taste, not to mention strong sense too: for all of which good things take us—you won't find one of them when you find . . . vulgarity.

Even with "the brush whisked out of my grasp," he gave himself the background training of a painter, and instead of classical literature

(Brownell takes him to task for the lack) it was classical art which gave him those "impressions" his father had taught were "the dearest things in the world."

The museum world of twenty-five stories out of a total thirty of the early period is valuable not because its mechanics set up and resolve plots, or because its situational complexity—its art-making, art-watching, art-collecting—created "type" cleavages (the artist, the amateur, the collector, each classifiable into defective, excessive, and perverted). Its chief service is to determine certain fixed modes of experience permitted in the presence of art and under its aegis. The high art of Europe can be a terrible god if violated, a benevolent god if properly worshipped. The application of this dogma distinguishes the heroes or high priests from the failures or heretics. And it is significant that to the latter group belong the practising artists. Theobald of "The Madonna of the Future" fails because his overconcern with the secrets of Raphael paralyzes his hand. His is the talent that "can't act, that can't do or dare!" Roderick Hudson fails because "standing passive in the clutch of his temperament," he rejects the discipline of the masters: "he has no cleverness apart from inspiration." Our real failures in painting, Allston and Story, are the prototypes for the more imposing failures in the early fiction of James; the members of the American colony in Rome are probably models for Singleton, the plodding machine; Gloriani, the meretricious realist; and Miss Blanchard who only "did backs very well." The one permitted exercise of temperament is the rupture with an iconoclastic Puritan background. When European art is first presented to Mary Garland, she realizes the gulf between its world and that of her New England values: "To enjoy, as you say, these things is to break with one's past and breaking is a pain!" And her triumph over the values of her accustomed environment is her triumph in the novel: "Beauty . . . keeps saying that man was not made to suffer but to enjoy . . . I feel as if I were saying something sinful—I love it!"

The spectator of art avoiding sacrilege converts his impressions not into masterpieces manqués but into knowledge. From Giotto he learns how "to be *real;* real even as Giotto is real, to distinguish between genuine and factitious sentiment"; and although the nature of "the great emotion" is not always clear ("Is it art? Is it science? Is it sentiment? Is it knowledge? I am sure I can't say."), its effect is to "feel myself among scenes in which art had ranged freely; it had often been bad; it had never ceased to be great art." The apology for the apparent inertia of this life is made by Rowland Mallett, the real hero of *Roderick Hudson:* "A passive life in Rome, thanks to the number and quality of one's impressions, takes on a very respectable likeness to activity." The following dialogue between him and Mary Garland is a catechism for the art-lover:

> Is this what you call life? . . . all this splendour, all Rome; pictures, ruins, statues, beggars, monks?
>
> It's not all of it but it's a large part of it. All these things are impregnated with life; they're the results of an immemorial, a complex and accumulated, civilization . . .
>
> . . . which things have most beauty?
>
> That is according to taste. I should say the antique sculpture.

As long as one "never mistook the second best for the best" and "in the presence of a masterpiece . . . recognized the importance of the occasion," the question of the relative superiority of some of the works never arises. The "mystic meaning proper to themselves" is that they incorporate civilization at its best.

Civilization at its worst, on the other hand, is found in contemporary civilization, as *The American* illustrates. For Newman learns with some pain that "the crooked branch of an old family tree" may be confused with the great sights and great occasions. Poor Madame de Mauves, in the story of that name, out of excessive love for the great material past of Europe, marries a member of the French aristocracy whose "grossness . . . of imagination . . . was the same taste in essence . . . as the taste for M. Gerôme and M. Baudry in painting." His connection with the Europe of fine things is purely honorific. At this stage in James's Europeanization, Europe's best people measure up only to Europe's worst art. Until the appearance in 1881 of *The Portrait of a Lady* traditional art represents the only aspect of European civilization worth cultivating.

But with this book, the position itself is criticized. Although volume one, the complication, depends on accepting it, volume two, the dénouement, rejects it. The morality of the aesthetic life, if carried to its final conclusion, results in death of the spirit and stasis of action. Gilbert Osmond applies thoroughly Rowland's theory of aesthetic contemplation. Isabel's discovery that its practical application produces a monster harmful to the human items in his collection is conclusion through fable of James's own discovery that art for art's sake is injurious to life itself. The man who worships art exclusively will, in adjusting people to his museum scale of values, destroy their freedom. The *rigor mortis* produced by connoisseurship is prefigured before Isabel's discovery by a device possibly suggested to James by the novels of the de Goncourts and later developed in *The Golden Bowl.* Each character appended by Osmond to his collection is correlated with a work of art introduced at that point in the narrative when the character stands most in danger of being totally, partially, or potentially controlled by the aesthete. Pansy, his child, never had the chance to grow up as a person. Even her lover, Rosier, thought of her "in amorous meditation a good deal as he might have thought of a Dresden-china shepherdess," and the struggle to possess Pansy is a struggle for a piece of Kleinkunst. Madame Merle's partial subjection to Osmond is concretized by the image of a pot. She tells Isabel: ". . . even the hardest pots have a little bruise, a little hole somewhere. I flatter myself that I'm rather stout porcelain, but if I must tell you the truth, I've been chipped and cracked. I do very well for service yet because I've been cleverly mended." The repetition of this motif is reserved for that occasion when Madame Merle is in greatest danger of cracking up. "Please be very careful of that precious cup," she warns Osmond during a conversation with him in which her machinations seem to be turning out to no advantage either to Isabel or to herself.

> "It already has a small crack," said Osmond, dryly, as he put it down. . . . After he had left her, Madame Merle went and lifted from the mantel-shelf the attenuated coffee-cup in which he had mentioned the existence of a crack; but she looked at it rather abstractedly. "Have I been so vile all for nothing?" she murmured to herself.

The change from "pot" to "cup" shows that James never presses his symbols into a forced or mechanical service (something he criticized Hawthorne for in *The Scarlet Letter*), repeating them once, and in a slightly modified form. The image of "a gentleman in a pink doublet and hose and a ruff leaning against the pedestal of the statue of a nymph in a garden" which his Lancret offers Ralph as analogue to his own life of leisure, occurs once again, at that point where his tragic love for Isabel is made known to her in the form of a warning against Osmond. In his garden reclining "at the base of a statue of Terpsichore—a dancing nymph with taper fingers and inflated draperies, in the manner of Bernini"; the freedom of his école-galant life is contrasted with the future claustration of Isabel, "the portrait of a lady," within a Roman museum-house. In similar fashion the gallery or art-filled interior becomes a symbol for a way of life, rather than a generalized mise en scène. Action is free in the Touchett home, hampered in the Osmond palace; for only when art is confined to one part of the house, or one part of life, not the whole house or the whole of life, is the human will left intact. Although it is not until James revises *The Portrait of a Lady* that "the false colours, the sham splendour" of the hotel room are explicitly compared to "vulgar, bragging, lying talk," so that the very setting for Osmond's proposal objectively correlates his evil intentions, in the original edition the actual choice of the room's style and its full description at the particular moment within the drama underline the full irony of the situation.

That *The Portrait of a Lady* is not a temporary deflection but a real change in James's attitude to art is corroborated by his travel books that bridge the transition. *Portraits of Places* of 1883 criticizes the "Byronic, the Ruskinian, the artistic, poetic, aesthetic manner of considering this fascinating peninsula [Italy]" of the *Transatlantic Sketches* of 1874. Then, only as compared with bad contemporary religious mosaics, could the Byzantine mosaics of Ravenna be adjusted to the hierarchy of art values, for "they borrow a certain value from the fact that they are twelve or thirteen centuries less distant from the original." Then art gained prestige from the past. Now, in 1883, we find that art is great if it contains the present. Veronese is rated higher than Titian or Tintoretto, for "Never was a painter more nobly joyous, never did an artist take a greater delight in life." But how much greater than Veronese is Venice itself, for "all Venice was both painter and model. . . . Nowhere do art and life seem so interfused." In *A Little Tour in France* of the next year James no longer bothers to justify traditional art by its content of life. He goes directly to life itself, and with a summary glance at the cathedral, he glories in "that half hour in front of the café, in the mild afternoon, suffused with human sounds." "The most charming thing at Poitiers is simply the promenade of Blossac —a small public garden"—not the façade of Notre Dame la Grande. That same year he marries Verena of *The Bostonians* not to the Cambridge aesthete who "liked her for the same reason he liked old enamels and old embroideries," but to a backwoods lawyer who "had seen very few pictures; there were none in Mississippi. . . ."

The interesting fact of this reversed equation between the material and spiritual aspects of civilization is not that the "things" of traditional art have transmitted their power of regulating behavior to the society condemned in the Seventies, but that this society itself is valued only in so far as it is potential stuff for the traditional art of the future. In the fiction from 1884 to 1901 that area of life which is dignified by the attention of the painter alone can help define the limits for moral action. To select the best from the exhibited picture of contemporary life requires the accuracy of the professional vision. To preserve this best requires the formal product of an artist's vision, the painting. And so the work of art, secularized and contemporaneous, potential rather than actual, serves as a standard for judging human values, not in its shape as formal history, but in its shaping of formal life. This transmutation of the values of plastic art was not only a phenomenon of James's personal development. The artists of the Eighties were participating in a rebellion against the museum initiated by Monet and Renoir when they literally turned their backs on the Louvre to paint the life in the streets outside it. The artists in James's middle stories reflect the emphasis on the retinal field in their rating of the human eye above the traditional masterpiece as visual guide. These men succeed where Roderick and Theobald had failed, because they "pretended to be neither Raphael nor Leonardo"; they were merely "modern searchers." More often they use their eyes only to see in life some subtle secrets concealed from the nonprofessional eye by the conventions of society. They rarely paint. The young impressionist of "A New England Winter" "was of course very conscious of his eye; and his effort to cultivate it was both intuitive and deliberate. . . . It was not important that things should be beautiful; what he sought to discover was their identity—the signs by which he should know them," but he never takes a brush in hand. The nonpainting painter of "Mrs. Temperley" sees that Dora had been "formed to live in a studio, not in a stiff drawing room amid upholstery horribly new." The artist in "The Liar" calmly accepts the destruction of his picture, for his real job had been to reveal the sitter's concealed tendency to lie, and to watch it "grow and grow under his brush." Sight for the painter is insight, and during this period James's own insight is so fabled.

As the Story circle in Rome had provided the prototypes for the doomed painters of the early fiction, so John Singer Sargent and his group of Anglo-American fellow-artists were the models for the middle-period painters, and acquaintanceship with these men intensified James's interest in painting. Meeting Sargent with enthusiasm in 1884, by 1886 James had spent six weeks with him and Edwin Abbey, Frank Millet, and Alfred Parsons, sharing their studio life at Broadway, Worcestershire. The papers he wrote for *Harpers'* of this year in appreciation of these painters show the bias of his interest in their art. He understood painting only when it was convertible to literature, when its meaning emerged not through the autonomy of its formal relations but through the story implied in the choice of subject matter. The writer and painter both "record the immense field of contemporary life observed for an artistic purpose," their only distinction lying in the difference of their tools:

> If one has attempted some such exploit in a literary form, one cannot help having a sense of union and comradeship with those who have approached the question with the other instrument. This will be especially the case if we happen to have appreciated that instrument even to envy.

This identification of the aims of fiction with those of illustration extends to his comments on painting, and makes his criticism of the latter commonplace and traditional. He tends to summon up acknowledged masters as standards for contemporary work, and his enthusiasm for Sargent's portrait of "a young girl, engaged in the casual gesture of holding up a flower" leans for authority on the recollection of Velasquez. Those characteristics which connect

Sargent with the avant-garde painting of his time, James feels betray "the latent dangers of the impressionist practice . . . ; tendency to simplification and the neglect of a certain faculty for lingering reflection." *El Jaleo* "has the quality of an enormous 'note' or memorandum, rather than of a representation." For a writer who felt that "a picture without composition slights its greatest chance for beauty," and that "there is no greater work of art than the portrait," the segmental composition of the orthodox Impressionists and their tendency to rate landscape above the portrait would be unwarrantable breaks with tradition. His most glaring critical error, in a field he never really understood other than as metaphor for writing, is the ranking of Gavarni above Daumier, who left out "so much of life—youth and beauty and charm of women and the loveliness of children . . . and the manners of those social groups of whom it may be said that they *have* manners." His raptures over Du Maurier stem from his delight in the people he draws, not from what James calls "a quality of observation which is new in the world." When he transfers pictorial terms to literary criticism the effect as metaphor is valid. In the essay on Howells written the same year as his art criticism, 1886, he appreciates the "work of observation, of patient and definite notation," regretting, however, the failure sometimes to "paint, to evoke the conditions and appearances, to build in the subject." And his wish expressed to Stevenson in 1888 "to leave a multitude of pictures of my time, projecting my small circular frame upon as many different spots as possible" begins this metaphorical habit which was to continue to the end of his career.

At the close of the decade James's attention settles on the doing of the picture, rather than on the seeing of the subject. The scenes, therefore, become less populated, the number of the characters contracts and the donnée is to justify the solitary application of the painter to his art by the worth of the *done* result. *The Tragic Muse,* 1890, meets the typically British objection to art as something "pardonable as long as it's done at odd hours" by proving that it represents the most serious and productive activity. If the life of impressions lived by Gabriel Nash has neither form nor permanence, if the life of politics lived by Sherringham has permanence but no form, if the life of the stage lived by Miriam Rooth has form but not permanence, that life which has both form and permanence is the painter's, for he makes the "thread on which the pearls of history (the great portraits) are strung." As long as Nick Dormer formalizes history in art, he is as important as Raphael. The "mystic meaning" proper to art is that it embodies the best of civilization, not of the past but of present life, and man's proper relation to it is creative: he gives it new forms. The painter of "The Real Thing" finds that the real aristocrats are useless models for their "type," since they leave no room for the artist's recreative gift.

In 1892 James writes in a letter to Charles Eliot Norton: *"Painting* . . . it is true I have ceased to feel it very much." From now on he rarely uses the fable of the painter and, when he does, it is to illustrate a general principle which he has abstracted from the special case. Life is capable of assuming form, and drama consists of the interaction between those who impose and those who accept form. *The Spoils of Poynton* shows the plastic sense diverted by a mother from her son to her furniture, producing a beautiful house and a boorish son. The spoils and Owen are respectively the formed and unformed results of a mother's attention, and their basic unity explains why Fleda Vetch cannot possess even one small piece of the spoils when she has lost their human counterpart. James parallels the burning of the spoils with Owen's marriage, that stage where he ceases to be his mother's material. *What Maisie Knew* and *The Awkward Age* demonstrate how plastic youth can assume monstrosity of form when molded to the advantage of sinister occasions. The volume entitled *The Two Magics* presents in two stories both the evil and good effects of the instinct for form: the possession by evil agents of "the helpless plasticity of childhood that isn't dear or sacred to *some*body" is the theme of "The Turn of the Screw." "Covering End" shows the magical effects the plastic gift bestows on an old house and its exploited owner shaping them into beauty and character.

What *The Portrait of a Lady* is to the early fiction, *The Sacred Fount,* 1901, is to the middle. This book is not "a parody of James's novels of intelligence," as Mr. Matthiessen believes, but a serious rejection of an attitude to art on which the fiction of the Eighties and Nineties is based. It implies that the artist cannot reach "the deeper psychology," since the locus of his observation is the surface of human beings. The personal application of art as doing ("because I am that queer monster, the artist . . . ," writes James much later to Henry Adams, "It all takes doing—and I *do*.") in the solitary years at Rye followed "the painter sense deeply applied" to its logical limits. A visitor at a house party assumes from the appearance of four people that two of them are draining the life force from two others. The problem is to sort out the victims, and with an artist fellow-guest, he launches on an exhaustive attempt to fit the people into his scheme. But a mature adult is plastic not by accident but by will, and the secret of the form he may have assumed is revealed not to the prying outsider but to someone actually engaging in the experience. Even the picture of "a man with a mask," pressed into the service of the revelation, can give no clues, for there is no link between it and the actors of the private drama. When Mrs. Brissendon calls the visitor mad (the painter has already given up the search), she implies that only through the consciousness of one of the participants of the intrigue itself can the viewer reach the springs, "the sacred fount," of human behavior. This novel introduces the late fiction in which situations are revealed only through the actual consciousness of one or more of the characters.

Now only direct experience can ultimately guide moral action, but just as the fiction of the middle period retained some of the values of the early period in which traditional art dominated, so the knowledge of the middle stories, the capacity of life to accept form, functions as accessory to experience directly felt. It helps create the données of the last period which recapitulate those of James's entire career. For Chad is Madame de Vionnet's product, as Millie is Kate Croy's, as the Prince is Adam Verver's, but only up to the point where as intelligent human beings they will accept these roles. The failure of form to contain them, in fact, contributes to their story.

The late works offer a final balancing of the two phases of Europe as civilization: rare art and rare life. As art dictated to behavior in the early fiction, and life dictated to art in the middle fiction, the final adjustment is a reconciliation between them. As furies turned into Eumenides, the spoils of Europe, its traditional art, return as the handmaidens, not the enemies of experience. But it is not the great masterpiece of the museum that comes back, for its relation to experience is too remote; nor is it the contemporary portrait of a person in the drama. (James in three stories of 1902 exhausted this possibility: "The Beldonald Holbein" is a verbal and pictorial pun; "The Tone of Time" and "The Special Type" show portraits serving as substitutes for people.) The works of art of the final stories have value as rare things, but they function first not as items in private collections but as clues to the motives and drives of the people to whom they are addressed and for whose use they are disposed. The "mystic meaning proper to themselves" is the moral tone of the life they are saturated with. Strether realizes one part of Madame de Vionnet's effect on Chad when he sees the taste for fine things which she had developed in him, but he only grasps her intrinsic value when he receives impressions from the "things" in her own home, possessions superior to those of either Chad or Miss Gostrey. Those two:

> had rummaged and purchased and picked up and exchanged, sifting, selecting, comparing; whereas the mistress of the scene before him, beautifully passive under the spell of transmission . . . had only received, accepted and been quiet. . . . At bottom of it all for him was the sense of her rare unlikeness to the women he had known. . . . Everything in fine made her immeasurably new, and nothing so new as the old house and the old objects.

The form of Strether's knowledge of her value is presented through the formal aspects of her personality, her possessions, and through them the chief of *The Ambassadors* accepts the discovery of what in Woolett morality is an indecent, but in civilized morality may be a "virtuous," relationship. This is the knowledge Strether brings to America, and all he can regret is that the experience itself was denied him.

In *The Wings of the Dove* art objects again are instrumental in revealing human motives to those whose intelligence can penetrate this "mystic meaning." Densher senses that Mrs. Lowder is a symbol of brute force which makes the life force, Kate, subject innocence, Milly, to exploitation. He reads it in "the huge, heavy objects that syllabled his hostess' story."

> It was the language of the house itself that spoke to him, writing out for him, with surpassing breadth and freedom, the associations and conceptions, the ideals and possibilities of the mistress.

At every stage Densher measures the personality against the material accumulations made by that personality. Unfortunately, his own seduction by Kate keeps him from applying the message of these things to the facts of the crime. But in the end the pieces of furniture of Kate's family help him to realize the truth:

> Whatever might have been itself the quality of these elements Densher could feel the effect proceeding from them . . . to be ugly almost to the point of the sinister. They failed to accommodate or compromise; they asserted their differences without tact and without taste. . . . It was truly having a sense of Kate's quality thus promptly to see them in reference to it.

Through apparent contrast to her sister's interior decoration, Kate is ironically characterized. The book closes on "the shabby things" as it had opened on them, resolving Kate's behavior in terms of actual motivation. Milly, on the other hand, compensates for her failure to live by a retreat to the world of traditional art:

> She wouldn't let him call it keeping quiet, for she insisted that her palace—with all its romance and art and history—had set up round her a whirlwind of suggestion that never dropped for an hour. . . . Hung about with pictures and relics, the rich Venetian past, the ineffaceable character, was here the presence revered and served. . . . Millie moved slowly to and fro as the priestess of the worship.

Venice as the richest form of the past protected her with its art and with its patron saint, Lord Mark, who had revealed to her through the Bronzino portrait (a work of the past) the image of her possibilities.

If Milly, "the heiress of all the ages," could possess Europe only through its art, its life passing her by, Adam Verver of *The Golden Bowl* finally possesses Europe in its material form as art and its spiritual form as personality. The price he must pay is the sacrifice of his innocence, his Americanism. ("American life is, on the whole, as I make no doubt whatever, more innocent than that of any other country," James had written in 1886.) He must submit to experience. There are two main myths which can be extracted from what James in his preface calls "the gathered cluster of all the *kinds* of interest." One, the myth of the discovery by the new world (innocence) and the old world (experience) of each other, operates only in key metaphors in the consciousness of the characters. Adam, the new world, compares himself to the discoverer Cortez rifling "the Golden Isles," even subconsciously using the legend of Cortez' burning of his ships, when he proposes to Charlotte. Amerigo, the Prince, in "discovering the Americans," enters his "port of the Golden Isles" in the image of Vespucci, his ancestor. Subsidiary images reinforce this opposition of innocence to experience: Adam is the "natural fowl running round the basse-cour"; Amerigo is "cooked down as a crème de volaille"; Adam is the first man living the life of innocence and ignorance in the "state before the Fall." The Prince is "steeped" in history "as in some chemical bath." The opposition in this basic myth provides the necessary motivation for the overt myth, that of the American's view of Europe's civilization, both art and life, as objects for a collection. For the Cortez complex in Adam takes the form of art patron with such intensity that the Prince becomes a crystal; Charlotte, Oriental tiles; and even his daughter, some "draped antique of Vatican or Capitoline halls." Parallel to this effect the Prince's Vespucci complex determines the elements of his experience as colored by what he receives as his end of the bargain in presenting himself as a morceau de musée—money! Charlotte for him is "some long, loose purse well filled with gold pieces," her words of assignation "the chink . . . of gold in his ear," their day together "some great gold cup." These two myths are joined on the level of action by an object of art itself, a golden bowl, which, first a symbol of Amerigo's and Charlotte's adultery, becomes a symbol of the Ververs' deformed attitude to their precious people. For when people are treated like works of art, certain human needs are ignored which will eventually assert themselves and turn the tables on those who possess them. Thus Amerigo and Charlotte, in their private intrigue, actually "fixed" Maggie and Adam. The bowl, therefore, as a real symbol of an unnatural point of view, is broken by Mrs. Assingham, the Greek chorus who interprets the real meaning of experience to both the characters of the drama and to the reader. When Maggie and Adam at the end of the novel review their possessions, they know that to deserve them they must accept all of the experience which they contain, its good and evil. The possession of rare objects is only assured when their complex human values are understood. The "mystic meaning proper to themselves" of the spoils of Europe is that they incorporate all the values of experience, and must be understood through experience itself.

The two incomplete novels that close James's career indicate how far he might have carried this ratio of art to life. In *The Sense of the Past* a writer shows how far sympathy for the life contained in objects can carry him. The contact of his past-filled imagination with the past-filled objects resurrects history itself. However, once submerged in it Ralph Pendril realizes that the past is of value only when viewed through the present. For it is only because he has never lost a psychic connection with his own time that he can climb back into it. The notes indicate that Pendril will finally occupy the house with its historical relics, but as a man of the twentieth century. In *The Ivory Tower* James reverses this situation by submerging a man of traditional training in the society of the future, America, from which he escapes figuratively and literally through the aid of an ivory tower. This tower, although a material thing, is actually less material than the society he flees. This late use of the art object as talisman, capable through the saturation of its form with life of representing it, illustrates the point that James is never eccentric to his period but parallels in his thought and iconography the changes at work in certain habits of the imagination. At the end of the century there was a reaction to the view of an art object as the product of the visually professional confrontation of the natural scene. The object was now valued not as a mirror but as a contrast to life. For since the life coming within the retinal field was now mechanical, vulgar, industrial, the object valued was traditional, decorative, and mysterious. The golden bowl receives its gilt from the hand of "a very fine old worker and by some beautiful process." Its actual provenience is ambiguous, as is the ivory tower's, about which little is known except that it "was a remarkable product of some eastern, probably some Indian, patience, and of some period as well when patience in such causes was at the greatest." And when the Bronzino in *The Wings of the Dove* and the ancestor portrait in *The Sense of the Past* become agents of the peripety of action, one invokes Wilde's *Dorian Grey* rather than Hawthorne.

Whether his particular action of the works of art indicates that James was a religious personality working in a period when he could find his only absolute, "the substance of things hoped for," in the great art of plastic representation, or whether it reveals him as the American most sensitive to the struggle of his countrymen to possess a complex civilization, of one thing we can be sure: of all the writers of his period who attempted the problem, he alone has made a complete record of that struggle.

# The Political Vocation

*by Irving Howe*

Henry James is a novelist of temptations, temptations resisted, succumbed to, regretted; but the temptation of politics, which has haunted so many modern writers, seems never to have troubled him at all. Politics could rarely excite him to intense emotion or problematic thoughts; he never seems to have regarded it as a human activity with a value, or at least a necessity, of its own. To the degree that it did figure in his world, James was a conservative, though less in formal opinion than as a tangle of what might be called cultural emotions:—a hushed reverence before the great things of the past which had been wrenched from the endless blood and failure of history; a feeling that history being what it was these great things were probably inseparable from the blood and the failure; a distaste for the vulgarity of public life, which had been one reason for quitting America, where life was strenuously public; and a deep distrust, indeed a professional refusal, of abstract ideas. As a writer with a marvelous gift for making the most of his disabilities, James never had to face the question—except, perhaps, toward the very end of his life—whether such attitudes were an artist's privilege or the mark of that American innocence which would remain with him to the end of his life in Europe. He did not have to face such questions because he lived at a time when it was still possible for a writer like himself to make of conservatism a personal aesthetic value rather than a mere ideology.

Unlike Dostoevsky, James had never been singed by radicalism,

"The Political Vocation." (Originally entitled "Henry James: The Political Vocation.") From *Politics and the Novel* by Irving Howe, pp. 139-156. 

though he had seen it flickering in his father's Fourierist circle and burning in his sister Alice's mind; unlike Conrad he felt no need to discipline or suppress memories of a family tradition of political revolt. James's conservatism was peculiarly the conservatism of an artist who has measured all the effort and agony that has gone into the achievements of the past and is not ready to skimp their value in the name of an unborn and untested future. And it was the conservatism of a man with a profound sense of human disability, an awareness of catastrophe and failure so great as at times to be crippling in its power. So that when he came to write about nineteenth century revolutionary politics in *The Princess Casamassima*, his own opinions were neither risked nor challenged; the book presented itself to him as an experiment in craft and imagination: how well could he survey an area of life he had never explored? In the preface he would later write for the novel he acknowledged this problem bravely, in the novel itself somewhat less so.

*The Princess Casamassima* fascinated him as a virtuoso flight—or descent—to the world of anarchist London in the 1880's, a world that had recently been brought to anxious public attention by the Trafalgar Square riots. Whatever was unknown, shadowy and fearful in the idea of a radicalism churning beneath the surface of London stimulated his curiosity; he wished to seize upon the potential of destruction while it remained a mere potential ("the sick, eternal misery crying out of the darkness in vain") and to dramatize it against the grimy backdrop of the London slums. It was an exercise in the sheer power, the grasping power, of intelligence to divine that which it did not really know.

"I have never yet become engaged in a novel," he confided to his notebook, "in which, after I had begun to write . . . the details remained so vague." Nor was this vagueness quite the pondered choice he would later claim in his preface when he spoke of "Our not knowing, of society's not knowing, but only guessing and suspecting and trying to ignore, what 'goes on' irreconcilably, subversively, beneath the vast smug surface." Still, there is something admirable in James's creative bravado, his boldness in summoning the unknown and his economy in exploiting his ignorance; there is something even more admirable in his readiness to face the possibility—he seems to have thought it a likelihood—that the society to which he was committed by taste and habit was on the edge of disaster. For if it was James's conscious intention in writing *The Princess Casamassima* to discover how far he could extend the powers of his art into an unfamiliar subject, he was also moved by more intimate needs. The book registered his fear that everything he valued was crumbling, and it would be gratuitous to question the depth or sincerity of this fear; but it also betrayed his doubt whether, in some ultimate moral reckoning that was beyond his grasp, everything did not deserve to crumble. This could hardly affect his conservative temper, which by now had become thoroughly ingrained, but it did permit him an openness and breadth of feeling greater than is usually available to those in whom conservatism is merely an opinion.

*The Princess Casamassima* is a bewildering mixture of excellence and badness. It sets up at least three main lines of action: the personal faith of Hyacinth Robinson, the career of the Princess, and the activities of the revolutionists, particularly Paul Muniment. Strictly in "technical" terms, the novel suffers from James's failure sufficiently to work these three strands into one another, so that they often seem to be parallel when they should be interwoven. But as one might expect, this "technical" failure is a sign of some deeper failure in conception, indicating that while James was able to imagine, brilliantly for the Princess and indulgently for Hyacinth, the tone and quality of each part, he was weak at connection, at relating one to the other—that is, at precisely the point where general ideas become indispensable *for this kind of novel.*

It is the Princess herself who is the great triumph of the book, the one figure whom James has filled in with avid completeness and with regard to whom it is impossible, except at the very end, to cavil. She is one of a type that was first beginning to appear in James's day and has since become entirely familiar: the woman of superior energies to whom society can offer neither secure place nor proper work, the woman who finds it not enough to be feminine or even female yet cannot establish herself in independence from her sex. She has pushed herself—or rather, if we remember *Roderick Hudson,* the novel in which she first appeared, she has been pushed —to the summits of society, and finds the conquest not worth the candle: it offers no outlet for her large vague talents; if the lower world is drab, the upper is tedious. James knew her type intimately, she was peculiarly the product of the Anglo-American set; he understood her in every respect, including the degree to which sheer sexual boredom can drive such a woman to both fantasy and frenzy.

In his preface he applied three descriptives to her and they are exactly right: she is "the fruit of restless vanity," a woman who would be more than a woman yet knows not what; she displays a conspicuous "aversion to the banal," so that her expedition through society is first a quest for the picturesque and then for the thrilling; and she is "world-weary," her triumphs have come too cheaply. The Princess Casamassima is James's "heroine of all the ages" in her aspect of ugliness, as Isabel Archer from *The Portrait of a Lady* is that heroine in her aspect of loveliness. At times—I suspect the critics miss the snicker that comes from the future Lion of Lamb House—at times she is a creature of high comedy; James is more than a little malicious when he has her say to Hyacinth upon his arrival in her country home: "I wish you had come in the clothes you wear at work." The buzz of pitying solemnity which James affixes to poor little Hyacinth should not be allowed to obscure the fine comedy of the Princess picking Hyacinth's intellectual pocket, quavering before Muniment's delicious because proletarian coarseness, and saturating herself in Bloomsbury dinginess in order to prove she is a serious revolutionary.

There is another, more personal note: the Princess knows that her status, even as far as purchased nobility goes, is false, merely the result of an evil marriage engineered by an adventurous mother. She is in the intolerable position of suspecting that all social currencies may be counterfeit and of wondering whether anyone—be it Hyacinth or Muniment or even the shadowy Hoffendahl—can provide her with a genuine piece of newly minted revolutionary silver. At a time when the characteristic social climber in the English novel was still laboriously making her way up, following the calculated footsteps of Becky Sharp, James realized that the really interesting and troublesome climbers had begun to hurry down.

When the Princess invites the dispossessed little bookbinder to be her houseguest—it is a fine point, incidentally, which she considers the more piquant, his radicalism or his gentlemanliness—she intends it as a deliberate gesture of defiance:

> How little the Princess minded—how much indeed she enjoyed the consciousness that in having him about her in that manner she was playing a trick on society, the false and conventional society she had sounded and despised—was manifest from the way she had introduced him to the group they found awaiting them in the hall on the return from their drive. . . .

But the Princess' rather flashy contempt for her own class is not justified or balanced by warmth of feeling toward any other class. She is interested in revolution or at least the idea of revolution, but not in the wretched human beings in whose name the revolution is presumably to be made. There is a neatly arranged incident in the novel where Hyacinth takes her on a mild slumming expedition to a public bar and the Princess reveals her fundamental hardness:

> The softer sex . . . was embodied in a big hard red woman, the publican's wife, who looked as if she were in the habit of dealing with all sorts and mainly interested in seeing whether even the finest put down their money before they were served. The Princess pretended to "have something" and to admire the ornamentation of the bar; and when Hyacinth asked her in a low tone what disposal they should make, when the great changes came, of such an embarrassing type as that, replied off-hand, "Oh, drown her in a barrel of beer."

And even when the Princess indulges in charity—for James is relentless in tracking down her motives—Hyacinth must admit to himself that "her behavior, after all, was more addressed to relieving herself than to relieving others."

As she breathlessly wonders whether the revolution is "real" or not, whether it is a "gathering force" or a "sterile heroism," the Princess becomes a prototype of the upper-class fellow-traveler, a wicked anticipation of the kind of woman who comes to politics searching for experience she can find nowhere else. She is a cousin of Dostoevsky's Varvara Petrovna, but only a distant cousin. For where Varvara Petrovna would peer into the "gathering force," she would plunge into it; and where Varvara Petrovna would yesterday have given cocktail parties, she would today be stealing atom secrets.

It would be a great mistake, and a slighting of James's originality, to think of the Princess as simply an idle woman amusing herself with the idea of radicalism. To suppose that would be to underestimate the explosive power of boredom in modern society, as well as the distance to which the hunger for "the real thing" can take such people. The Princess is a woman of desperate possibilities; one believes entirely in her willingness and capacity to assume Hyacinth's terrorist mission. But if one does credit the Princess' affinity for desperation, it follows that James made a bad mistake in intimating at the end of the novel, through the person of Muniment, that she would return to her moldy prince for lack of money. On the contrary. Everything James has himself shown us of the Princess, and shown us so superbly, indicates that she would not hesitate to go deeper, to take poverty as still another *experience,* and give herself completely to revolutionary or what she supposed to be revolutionary activities. The only damper upon her enthusiasm would perhaps be her discovery that revolutionary politics, instead of bursting into a gorgeous total insurrection, required patient and undramatic preparation. But while she might abandon the anarchists—in time even they might not seem vigorous enough for her—the Princess would not return to her past, she would blunder ahead into the unknown: desperate, searching, grasping. Above all, grasping.

## II

How well James guessed, for he did not know, some of the surface qualities of nineteenth century anarchism, Lionel Trilling has noted in his essay on *The Princess.* With instinctive tact James placed his action on Sundays, the one day of the week workers were then likely to have free for politics—and he must surely have appreciated the irony in this exchange of ritual pieties. The anarchists are cast, correctly enough, as skilled artisans rather than factory proletarians. And the bursts of discontent that fill the air of the primitive radical gatherings at the Sun and Moon Café ("What the plague am I to do with seventeen bob—seventeen bloody bob?", "Well, are we in earnest or ain't we in earnest—that's the thing *I* want to know") are credible enough in their uncouthness and aimlessness.

All this rings true, one is ready to call upon one's little fund of knowledge to attest to its truth; but James was offering little more than fragments of insight, splinters of observation, shrewd guesses. Inevitably, some of the guesses proved to be wrong. George Woodcock, an English critic thoroughly familiar with the history of anarchism, has written a sympathetic account of the novel in which he remarks that "James shows merely a knowledge of the kind of distorted rumours and journalistic stories by which [the anarchists] were represented in the newspapers of the late nineteenth century." Mr. Woodcock points out that the anarchist movement actually consisted of "a loose collection of individuals and groups devoted to spontaneous direct action and personal propaganda rather than conspiracy," and that "an authoritarian circle of conspirational leaders, such as James imagines in *The Princess Casamassima,* was wholly inconsistent with . . . the doctrines and the very name of Anarchism."

This correction is important not because it proves that James drew an inaccurate picture of anarchism, for surely no one would today be troubled on that score, but because it supports the opinion that James, despite many fine touches, was relying far too comfortably on his celebrated lack of knowledge and justifying far too easily his acceptance of secondhand impressions. The result was a novel in which the most brilliant insights into political character jostle a view of politics that reminds one, a little uncomfortably, of the catchwords of melodramatic journalism.

There are times when *The Princess Casamassima* seems almost designed to evade its own theme. Everything is prepared for but little is revealed, doors open upon doors, curtains onto curtains. The elaborate skirmishing around the central brute fact of the novel—I mean, of course, the nature and power of social radicalism—is probably due to James's hesitation at taking it firmly in hand as he had taken other subjects in hand. He is skittish in his treatment because he is uncertain of his material; and he is uncertain of his material not merely because he does not know it intimately, but more important, because he vaguely senses that for a subject so explosive and untried something more is needed than the neatly symmetrical laying-out of his plot or the meticulous balancing of his characters. But what that might be, he does not know.

James tries very earnestly to accumulate sensuous impressions of the London slums; and there are passages in which he bears down hard, turning to an elaborate rhetoric not very common at this stage of his career, in order to convey through eloquence what he does not quite manage through dramatization.

> They came oftener this second winter, for the season was terribly hard; and as in that lower world one walked with one's ear nearer the ground the deep perpetual groan of London misery seemed to swell and swell and form the whole undertone of life. The filthy air reached the place in the damp coats of silent men and hung there till it was brewed to a nauseous warmth, and ugly serious faces squared themselves through, and strong-smelling pipes contributed their element in a fierce dogged manner which appeared to say that it now had to stand for everything—for bread and meat and beer, for shoes and blankets and the poor things at the pawnbroker's and the smokeless chimney at home.

If only because such passages indicate how superbly conscious James was of his handicap and how genuine was his sympathy toward the speechless suffering poor who hover in the background of the novel, they are often admirable; yet one cannot suppress the feeling that, for all their local persuasiveness, these bursts of high generalization are there to deflect attention from James's trouble in working out his theme. Precisely in those sections—the sections dealing with the political world—where the novel should be most dense, it is most porous. And again, this failure is not merely the "technical" one of being unable to populate an alien world; it points to another, more serious failure which can be understood only by examining James's treatment of his radical characters.

Taken one by one, they seem entirely successful. Eustache Poupin, veteran of the Paris Commune and the revolution of 1848, "a Republican of the old-fashioned sort . . . infinitely addicted to fraternity and equality," is a perfect specimen of the pre-Marxist but post-Jacobin revolutionary, shown in all his idealism, mental softness and *Schwärmerei.* An amiable blusterer who cannot shed his native respectability—his creed is that of Louis Blanc, his manners those of a French burgler—Poupin is a man of good will but moral sloth, a revolutionist of enthusiasm who is blind to the possibility that enthusiasm can also lead to murder. Poupin is not a very deeply imagined figure, his major function in the novel being to fail Hyacinth, and long before the need arises we know that he *will* fail Hyacinth; but within these limits he serves efficiently. Schinkel, the schematic German comrade, moves in the shadows of the book rather than its forefront, but he is a far more subtly conceived and realized figure than Poupin. He too, I cannot help noticing, seems to spring from the immediacy of radical experience: the lonely phlegmatic bachelor who fumbles through a routine of shabby order, with a perpetual bandage round his neck, a pipe for companion and the movement as breath and blood of life. Schinkel's feelings for Hyacinth go deeper than Poupin's, and so does his betrayal. He does not burble over the bewildered little artisan in the manner of the Frenchman but watches him from a distance, with longing and affection; and when it is he who is assigned to inform Hyacinth of the terrorist mission—for the Schinkels of this world are always trustworthy—he feels far more poignantly than Poupin the dilemma of their young friend. He protests to Hyacinth that he "lofes" him, and it is true, he "lofes" him; yet he fulfills his part of the mission with precise loyalty. Schinkel is one of those Jamesian "reverberators" who takes everything in, who feels it all intensely, so that only at the very end do we grasp the full extent of his responsibility and his betrayal. The final sentence of the book is given to Schinkel's reflection that the revolver with which Hyacinth has killed himself "would certainly have served much better for the Duke." The weight assigned these words by their place in the novel, like the powerful grinding irony they enforce, falls back upon Schinkel in his role as representative figure of the anarchist world.

At no point in his invasion of that world is James bolder than in his handling of Paul Muniment, the minor anarchist leader; yet one might well complain that finally he is not bold enough. Muniment is a precise outline—there is more contour than substance—of the bureaucratic personality, in one variation the Labor Party parliamentarian and in another variation the Stalinist functionary. Since Muniment seldom troubles to develop his ideas, it is not possible to specify the precise shade of his bureaucratic ambition; but given the rudimentary state of the radicalism to which he has attached himself, this can hardly be seen as a serious fault in the novel. More troublesome is the fact that the interest created in him is disproportionate to the picture given of him. He is too prominent for a minor character and too shadowy for a major one. Though in some ways the most interesting and original figure in the book, we are kept at too great a distance from him and do not experience the full force of his political career. We see it only in its impact on a few of his friends, in his kindly manipulation of Hyacinth and his comic but ruthless struggle with the Princess for personal domination.

Up to a point James's vagueness with regard to Muniment's political life can be justified as part of a strategy for stressing fearful possibilities by refusing to choose among them—a strategy he inherited, of course, from Hawthorne. But once the political thread begins to color the novel, which is to say, about halfway through, Muniment should be filled in, if only to make more vivid and substantial one of the forces acting upon Hyacinth. This inadequacy, as I take it to be, is very likely due to James's lack of that deep and intimate knowledge of English working-class life which appears to such advantage in D. H. Lawrence's early novels.

Nonetheless, Muniment represents one of James's great strokes of intuition. James caught, almost on the fly, the characteristic traits of the labor bureaucrat: his self-assurance, which seems to rest upon something more than power of intellect; his sense of destiny, reflected in and partly the result of his air of portentous secrecy; his middle-class Philistinism in matters of morals and taste; his cool hunger for power; and all the while, his genuine devotion to the cause. These are traits of leadership anxiously familiar to our time; Muniment's very name, taken from the Latin verb meaning to fortify, suggests both the strength and aloofness of his type. A socialist leader once said he wished to rise not above his class but with it: Muniment foresaw another possibility, he would rise *on* it.

## III

Remarkable as was James's insight into political personality, I think it reasonable to say that it does not quite come to a commanding vision of the political life. James showed himself to be brilliantly gifted at entering the behavior of political people, but he had no larger view of politics as a collective mode of action. He had a sense of the revolutionaries but not of the revolutionary movement—which might not have mattered had not the movement been at least as important a character in the novel as the individuals who composed it. He made the mistake of supposing that the whole was equal to a sum of its parts; that if you exhausted the radicals you had gotten at radicalism. He discovered, or thought he discovered, that envy is a major motive among radicals; but even if true, this would not be very illuminating if only because envy works in a great variety of human situations; it does not distinguish one politics from another. To understand a social movement, one must seek to approach it in objective terms, in terms that put aside, at least for the moment, the motives of individual participants and assign a weight and meaning to the group itself. And this James, with his trained inexperience in abstract thought, could not do.

I am not complaining, it had better be stressed, that James the person lacked an ideology, for this fact, if it is one, does not here concern us. My point is that some motivating idea about the revolutionary movement, be it valid or not, was indispensable for bringing into full play the energies that lay waiting in the novel; and James the writer not only lacked such an idea, he did not really grasp the need for it. The idea of which I speak need not be made explicit by the writer, and generally it is preferable that it not be; but it needs to be present as an assumption of what the revolutionary impulse means, what it will do for and to society. It needs to be felt as an unseen force behind the characters, behind the events, behind the very words. That it is not felt means that the politics of the novel remains partly unused. The ensuing loss, like the criticism I am making, is literary, not ideological; it is a loss *within* the book.

But a qualification is needed. For one can see in James's novel a central idea of a sort, an idea once extremely popular in England and France. Nineteenth century publicists liked to depict the political struggle between radicalism and conservatism as a clash between cultural barbarism and cultural refinement. Depending on the bias of a given observer, the barbarism might be seen as vigorously healthy or loutishly destructive, the refinement as the heritage of past greatness or an effete decadence.

In a study of Courbet, the art historian Meyer Schapiro has described a large allegorical painting, *L'Atelier,* in which this cultural dualism is given physical representation. "The painter presents around him in the studio his two worlds, at the right, the world of art . . . on the other side, the people in their homeliness, poverty and simple interests." [1] For Courbet this representation did not imply an inherent or terrifying opposition, since he believed that the world of art and the world of the people could be reconciled through the ethos of radical democracy. But for many writers and artists of the nineteenth century no such *rapprochement* seemed plausible, and the rising popular movements were often seen by them as a rude threat to the values of culture.

James absorbed this notion in *The Princess Casamassima,* perhaps a little too uncritically. For the cultural judgment of politics, if pushed too far, can be as trivial as the political judgment of culture, if pushed any distance at all, can be inhumane. An aristocracy of culture, threatened by the indifference of society and the ignorance of rising plebeian movements, is always tempted to mistake its immediate needs for the larger needs of humanity—though sometimes, of course, this is no mistake at all. And in James there is a tendency to judge the movement Hyacinth Robinson joins not as it is morally good or bad, socially creative or destructive, but as it impinges on a cultured sensibility; he is trying, that is, to judge a very complex human enterprise by standards that are both essential and insufficient, and the result is a kind of cultural insularity.

## IV

These weaknesses might have been overcome—or glossed over—if James had chosen as his hero a figure of strength who would impose himself on the political environment and transform it through the force of his will and intelligence. Hyacinth Robinson, however, is one of the most passive of James's heroes. He is a

[1] Meyer Schapiro, "Courbet and Popular Imagery," *Journal of the Warburg Institute,* IV, 3-4.

youth, writes James, "on whom nothing is lost," and that is true: one fully credits his talent for registering every nuance of moral chivalry or coarseness. But he is also a youth on whom nothing rubs off; a bastard by birth, he behaves as if he were immaculate in conception. It is his languorous passivity, far more than anything he actually says or does, that constitutes his snobbism. Hyacinth's is the snobbism of the young man who expects things, who waits not rapaciously but wistfully. His desires are pathetically modest, his sensibility is exquisite: how can one help feeling for and with him? That he yearns for the graces of the rich, that he loves the beauties of the evil world, that he is irked by the foulness of the slums and disgusted by the brutalities of the workers he had meant to inspire—only a prig would censure him too harshly for these deviations from his political faith. What is difficult to accept, however, and what finally renders Hyacinth a not very interesting hero, is the curiously feminine insularity of his character, his remarkable gift for being utterly uncontaminated by the world through which he glides.

Had it been James's intention so to cast Hyacinth, one could only regret the choice and applaud the achievement. But clearly his intention is something more; Hyacinth is one of the few characters with whom he seems to have a strong and, I would suggest, a disastrous identification. Hyacinth, says James in his preface, is supremely capable of profiting from all the glories of civilization yet "condemned to see these things from the outside." He is "the trapped spectator," the "poor sensitive gentleman" in a younger version, the fine intelligence which quails before the betrayals and vulgarity of the world. And one side of James is all too susceptible to this figure of pathos, the side of James which takes upon itself the fullest burden of handicap. James does not see what a solemn stick his young man can often be, and he compounds the trouble by identifying not with Hyacinth's temptations but with his refusals. He makes Hyacinth too innocent, not in terms of knowledge, for Hyacinth sees everything, but in terms of motive. Long on chivalry and short on impulse, Hyacinth thrives on renunciation the way heroes thrive on experience; he is too noble to be genuinely interesting and too pathetic to be tragic. In the end, Hyacinth becomes a projection of James's vulnerability.

Not, of course, that Hyacinth is without appetites. He keeps buzzing around the Princess and Millicent Henning, who is a kind of proletarian princess, and in a moment of enthusiasm even pledges his life to the cause. But from some fatal flaw of acquired gentility, he seems unable to act upon his desires: it is a case, I suppose, of a good man ruined by his better instincts.

As his experience widens and he learns to enjoy the Princess' country estate, Hyacinth is torn between a vision of elegance, in which the alloy of snobbism is not always distinct from the gold of culture, and an identification with the suffering millions, in which the indulgence of self-pity softens his wrath against injustice.

> When he himself was not letting his imagination wander among the haunts of the aristocracy and stretching it in the shadow of an ancestral beech to read the last number of the *Revue des Deux Mondes,* he was occupied with contemplations of a very different kind; he was absorbed in the struggles and sufferings of the millions whose life flowed in the same current as his and who, though they constantly excited his disgust and made him shrink and turn away, had the power to chain his sympathy, to raise it to passion, to convince him for the time at least that real success in the world would be to do something with them and for them.

As long as this tension continues, this "eternal habit of swinging from one view to another," the book preserves a certain vibrancy and life. In its second half, however, Hyacinth's yearning for beauty and his assumption that it is inseparable from a life of privilege leads him to a moral smugness which James does not really "see through" and, in fact, seems almost to approve. He can now say

> that want and toil and suffering are the constant lot of the immense majority of the human race. I've found them everywhere but haven't minded them. Forgive the cynical confession. What has struck me is the great achievements of which man has been capable in spite of them—the splendid accumulations of the happier few, to which doubtless the miserable many have also in their degree contributed.

In defense of Hyacinth, Lionel Trilling has argued that his later phase represents a positive access of knowledge, perhaps even wisdom: "he has learned something of what may lie behind abstract [political] ideals, the envy, the impulse to revenge and dominance." No doubt; but it does not seem to occur to Mr. Trilling, as it did not occur to James, that something equally bad may exist behind the abstract ideals of art to which Hyacinth is now so uncritically pledged. Culture, no less than politics, can harden into ideology.

Yet James is so marvelous an artist that he succeeds in salvaging something from the character of Hyacinth. Intermittently we see another Hyacinth, a Hyacinth who does not readily give himself to the abstract ideals of either politics or art, who knows there is a price to be paid for each advantage in life and is ready to pay it, who realizes both the fatal ambiguities of action and the equally fatal consequences of inaction. In Chapter XXXV, probably the best in the book, this Hyacinth moves into full view and is presented with a directness and firmness that stirs one to reflect on how marvelous a novel *The Princess Casamassima* might have been.

As the chapter opens, the moment of choice is approaching for Hyacinth, and never has he been less prepared to face it. Together with Muniment, he goes off on a radiant Sunday afternoon to a London park, and in the midst of the brimming promiscuous life of the city the two men achieve a sudden closeness. Hyacinth faces both ways, toward his political conscience and his aesthetic desire, toward the masses in whose suffering he has been drenched and the art whose radiance has suddenly overwhelmed him. This is the Hyacinth of whom James had given us an earlier glimpse when he wrote, "It might very well be his fate to be divided to the point of torture, to be split open by sympathies that had pulled him in different ways. . . ." And now, ruminating on this lonely, lovely Sunday afternoon, "he saw the immeasurable misery of the people, and yet he saw all that had been, as it were, rescued and redeemed from it: the treasures, the felicities, the splendours, the successes of the world."

In the dialogue that runs between them, Hyacinth begins with a provocation: he indulges in the usual jibe against doctrines of equality, that they foster "the selfsame shade of asininity." Muniment's parry is neat: "When those who have no start to speak of have a good one it's but fair to infer they'll go further. I want to try them, you know." Hyacinth cannot stand up to his logical friend, his aggressiveness evaporates, and he pleadingly answers:

"I don't want you to think I've ceased to care for the people. What am I but one of the poorest and meanest of them?" And it is here that Hyacinth becomes an almost archetypal figure. Torn between the claims of the future and the claims of the past, between a vision of human fraternity in a world not yet made and the tangible glories of the cultural edifice, he is now, for the first time and at a fearful cost, fully sensitive to the possibilities of life.

His conflict seems insoluble to him, as in a way it is: Paris or the Sun and Moon Café, the whole unmeasured gift of past greatness or the grim demands of the political vocation. Here James has come upon—I shall not even try to guess how, except to note that he knew only too well what it meant to live between two worlds—he has come upon a problem that lies at the very center of political life. Hyacinth is trapped in the heart struggle between beauty and necessity: he wants only to live, only to respond, but it is his very awareness of the unmediated clash between beauty and necessity that destroys him. The world, pressing upon him with its crushing weight, will not let him live; the conflict between taste and belief that has ripped apart his life now proves to be an illusory one. Whatever James has missed in Hyacinth's world, he has understood one thing with a grim finality: that for Hyacinth, as for many in the world like him, the very yearning for choice reveals the power of destiny.

# The Tales

*by Leon Edel*

In 1888, when James was forty-five and had produced the equivalent of a lifetime of fiction—some ten novels and half a hundred short stories—he explained to Robert Louis Stevenson that he wanted "to leave a multitude of pictures of my time, projecting my small circular frame upon as many different spots as possible." He was planning, he said, to go in both for quantity and quality, so that the stories would "constitute a total having a certain value as observation and testimony." This was an ambitious program; but between the year of his letter to Stevenson and the end of the first decade of the new century, he more than doubled the number of his tales as well as of his novels. In all he wrote one hundred and twelve tales.

He had from the first worked in the shorter form. Ten years of storytelling—in various lengths—preceded his first significant novel. And it was with a slender tale, about a spirited little American girl in Rome, that he made his enduring reputation. "Daisy Miller" was of the 1870's, and there was at least one masterpiece of the short form for each decade. "The Aspern Papers" was of the 1880's; "The Turn of the Screw" was of the 1890's, and "The Beast in the Jungle" came early in this century. From time to time he would collect a group of tales to form a volume; during some years he issued two or three, and on occasion he almost glutted his own market. But he never exhausted the backlog he had created in the magazines. His first collection, *A Passionate Pilgrim and Other*

"The Tales," by Leon Edel. General Introduction to *The Complete Tales of Henry James* (New York: J. B. Lippincott Company, 1962), edited by Leon Edel. Reprinted by permission of the J. B. Lippincott Company.

*Tales* of 1875, contained but six of the twenty-seven tales he had written by that time. He did not care to revive all of his tales: some he disowned as mere apprentice work. Others did not fit the scheme or tone of the given volume. As he advanced in life, his earlier volumes went out of print and were superseded by later collections. The largest group of his tales ever assembled by him were the fifty-two included in the "New York Edition" of his selected fictional writings—less than half of his short story total.

Since his death some thirty or forty of his tales have been shuffled and reshuffled in various editions. His stories are unusually long and editors have tended to choose the shortest. Only by assembling them in the order in which they were written, is it possible to see his development and growth in a form which he found a constant challenge and in which he achieved a singular mastery.

James defined his personal art of the novel in his late prefaces to the "New York Edition"; and in these he also defined, with great clarity, his theory of the short story. He preferred to speak of short narratives as "tales," and to use the French word *nouvelle,* which so many of his editors obstinately insist on translating as "short novel." The French *nouvelle* has always been a much more elastic form than the English or American "short story." It has had many great masters; and its appeal to James resided in its being of unprescribed length. It possessed always *a length proper to itself.* For this reason, he spoke of it as "the beautiful and blest *nouvelle.*" He deplored the general tendency of magazines to disregard questions of "organic" form, and to consider short stories in terms of their shortness—that is, to make them conform to some arbitrary word-count. This does not mean that he favored an undisciplined prolixity. What he believed in was "masterly brevity," as he put it, and even more—"the idea beautifully developed." This was possible only in the tale, as consecrated long ago in prose by Boccaccio and in poetry by Chaucer. The closest James was to come to the magazine requirements of his day was in two tales of five thousand words each. His average tale runs from ten to twenty thousand words. And there is one which exceeds fifty thousand. This explains why, as he advanced in his career, he found it increasingly difficult to place his stories in the magazines.

By modern standards, fifty thousand words would be considered a short novel. James however called the fifty-three-thousand-word "Turn of the Screw" a tale, and the fifty-eight-thousand-word *Reverberator* a short novel: and he explained with great clarity where the difference lay. There were, for him, two kinds of short narratives—the "anecdote" and the "picture." The anecdote, he said, was an account of "something that has oddly happened to someone." To remain an anecdote, it had to point directly to that person, and to keep him at the very center of the story. On occasion, an anecdote tended to acquire "a surface really much larger than the mere offered face of the work." By becoming a dramatic action, in which the "something that has oddly happened" to the hero or the heroine happens to other characters as well, the anecdote ceases to be itself. It has evolved into a short novel.[1] This is why *The Reverberator* was counted among the novels, and the ghost story among the tales.

The story which was a "picture" differed from the "anecdote" in that it was not susceptible of becoming a dramatic action. It was usually a composition in a small frame—a foreground, a background, a center of composition. "I rejoice in the anecdote," James said, "but I revel in the picture." He asked above all for recognition of "shades and differences, varieties and styles" instead of the "blank misery" in the Anglo-Saxon world of the measured and undefined tale, the rule of the word-count.

It is not easy to offer a general description of a landscape as highly individualized as that of Henry James's tales. He spoke of them as a family "quite organized as such, with its proper representatives, its 'heads,' its subdivisions, and its branches, its poor relations perhaps not least." The world of his tales is visual, plastic, analytical; as in his novels, it is large and leisurely and peopled by the civilized and the self-aware. It is a world of manners and problems in behavior; there is no violence; the emphasis is rather on intensities of feeling. The medium is often verbal irony, satire,

[1] The short novels of James are *Watch and Ward, The Europeans, Confidence, Washington Square, The Reverberator, The Spoils of Poynton, What Maisie Knew, The Sacred Fount,* and the two novelized plays, *The Other House* and *The Outcry*. By James's definition, all of the "short novels" in Philip Rahv's collection *The Great Short Novels of Henry James* must be called tales.

paradox. He is constantly experimental—that is, willing to search for new ways of telling his story. We can best divide his tales into "early, middle, and late," and attempt a broad characterization of each, while recognizing that there are bound to be exceptions and overlappings in the different periods.

The early tales contain a goodly amount of apprentice-work. James had been a student of method long before he began to write and in his first tale, published anonymously, he revealed a considerable awareness of the art of manipulating the reader, making him look in certain directions and listen to certain talk. He had a strong flair for dramatic dialogue. His apprentice tales told of failure in love, renunciation, the reticence of young men, the unfathomableness of young women, the general fickleness of the female sex. They are rather melancholy and romantic, as young tales can be and rather devoid of the later wit: they have a lugubrious atmosphere, for all their skill. The settings were generally American—salt-boxes and frame houses, the abundant greenery of the landscape, certain New York streets and houses, the aspect of Newport. From the first James painted minutely; and he was subtle and reflective. He was concerned not so much with plot, as with personal relations.

The tales of his middle period mark his emergence as a brilliant and witty observer of life on both sides of the Atlantic. They represent his discovery of his European-American subject; and his ability to render it in a high, dry, humorous light. There is an extraordinary play of intellectual humor as he shows Americans looking at Europe and Europeans looking at America. And his bemused and aloof observation of Anglo-American society seems to be a source of endless fascination to him. He studies its manners, its idiosyncracies, its codes, its decencies, its shabbinesses, its pathos. In his strictly "international" stories he is a chiding critic of American egalitarianism and "newspaperism": he describes the spittoons carefully arranged—as in parade formation—in the Capitol rotunda and the noisy aspect of American hotels, where the children roller skate in the corridors or lie asleep late in the evening in the big lobby armchairs, wholly unparented. On the subject of maternal laxity, the glorification of the child in America, he is as eloquent as any child psychologist of today. And when he discovers that the

British enjoy to excess these observations of his homeland, he promptly demonstrates his impartiality by describing British society: particularly the rudeness and arrogance of certain members of the British upper classes—"an aristocracy is bad manners organized" was one of his pointed aphorisms. James was a creator of maxims, and his epigrammatic style did him constant service in evoking the human picturesque. When it came to painting scenes he was unmatched in his precision and his genius for essential detail: Washington Street in Boston, snow-piled and jammed with horse-cars, lives for us again in his tales, as do the people within the large-windowed houses in Beacon Street; or in his unforgettable picture of "rotten row" in Hyde Park, which provides a perfect setting for the drama of Lady Barberina. His minute notations of English life surprised the English; he saw so much that they took for granted. In all his writings he kept a certain "distance" from his materials which his contemporary critics often remarked. If this faculty for holding himself aloof, for transferring his vision to an analytical observer, made at times for coldness, it gave James also a clarity undisturbed by irrelevant emotion.

A great part of the "natural history" of the American woman is written into the tales of the middle period. James studied her with a mixture of affection, awe, and profound mistrust. Whether he is describing the flattened out mother of Daisy Miller, or the irrelevant parents of the self-made Pandora Day, or the powerful "managerial" woman, he is concerned with the American male's tendency to idealize womanhood, glorify children, and to abdicate all human and civilized responsibility to the wife.

> "An American woman who respects herself," said Mrs. Westgate, turning to Beaumont with her bright expository air, "must buy something every day of her life. If she cannot do it herself, she must send out some member of her family for the purpose."

By this simple economy the husband is made aware that his dollars are put to constant use. His job in American life was simply to provide the dollars. James understood the power-driven matron—American or British—to the very tips of her manicured fingers. There is a simple little story, seldom reprinted, about a widow named Mrs. Temperly—the name is artfully suggestive—in which the hero, wishing to marry one of her daughters, watches her in full control of family, servants, and her Paris salon. He admires her; he wonders how she can accomplish so much, and with such ease. "And does she do it so well without a man?" he asks himself. "There must be so many details a woman can't tackle." For even when he counts the governess and the intimate friends, all he sees is a "multiplication of petticoats." Then it comes over him: "She *was* a man as well as a woman—the masculine element was included in her nature. He was sure that she bought her horses without being cheated, and very few men could do that."

The tales of the late period might, at first glance, have been written by someone else, so great a change has occurred. The story-teller's mood is profoundly altered—but not his temperament. With middle age his tales cease to be minutely descriptive. The discussion of manners and the behavior of American girls gradually disappears: the preoccupation with problems of conduct gives way to a study of states of feeling and of dilemmas of existence. He begins to probe the "unlived" life of his characters and to portray "poor sensitive gentlemen" who discover too late the price they have paid for their sensitivity and their insulation against the shock of experience. We might speak of these tales today as being in the "existential" mode. They partake of that "tragic vision" which so many critics have found in James, the essence of which is contained in the poignant exclamation of Prince Amerigo in *The Golden Bowl*—"Everything's terrible, *cara*—in the heart of man."

In the late years everything *was* terrible in the heart of man for Henry James; and yet for the elderly artist, the fascination of this terror and the need to explore it remained. At the same time his tragic insight did not supersede his sense of high comedy. His study of nightmare and terror was carried on in such tales as "The Altar of the Dead" and "The Beast in the Jungle," rejected by the magazines but celebrated today, in which James presented the consequences of extreme egotism and failures in spiritual sharing and showed men who have sealed their eyes to the world and the love around them. The late tales are studies of "predicaments"—this explains the titles of such volumes as *Embarrassments, Terminations* or *The Soft Side*—of individuals frustrated and defeated who arrive at the ultimate tragedy—that of helplessly knowing the emptiness of their past. These are the writings of a psychologist who no longer worried about external realism, because he knew the reality and power of inner experience. During the late 1890's he wrote his "tales of the quasi-supernatural and the gruesome," adding new dimensions to the ghostly tale, as the popularity of "The Turn of the Screw" attests. And at the same time, in a brilliant vein of satire, he brought into being a series of tales which displayed his unexhausted wit. These are his "tales of the literary life." They chide the public for its Philistinism toward art; they mock the blindness of critics; and they laugh at literary journalists and lion hunters in the drawing rooms. The literary tales make no pretence at reality: James kills off all his *personae* in "The Figure in the Carpet," and leaves the puzzled literary journalist still seeking the secret of Vereker's work. Or he creates a novelist who wants to be a best-seller, but who always succeeds in writing a "distinguished" book which does not sell; and describes how a lady novelist, who sells in the tens of thousands, dreams of being a distinguished failure. These are artificial comedies, or fables for critics, drawn with high good humor from Henry James's own rueful experiences. They are studies of stupidity and ignorance in public places; in them an old anger has been transmuted into urbane laughter, and a lesson in gentle and sauve "criticism of life."

By reading James's tales in their chronological order we can see the historian of manners, the psychologist, the civilized mind, and the profound moralist turning his "small circular frame" upon experience and doing this in a developing style. At the beginning there is a camera-like sharpness, all focus and clear image; at the end it becomes "impressionistic"; no hard lines are tolerated, and the great phrases and images reverberate like a tolling bell. "To me," said William Dean Howells long ago, "there is a perpetual delight in his way of saying things." Many readers have testified to this; James is one of the few modern writers who can be *re*read with pleasure. A single reading never exhausts the richness of his prose or the detail of his observation.

The world of his stories is peopled largely by the upper classes, the leisured of *The Better Sort* or *The Soft Side*. But his tales are not as limited as this statement would suggest. We find in them also schoolteachers and grocery clerks; artists' models and penny-liners; impoverished bohemians and dowdy dowagers, and families who jump their hotel bills from one resort to another. James was concerned not with classes of people, or their "station of life," so much as with their hopelessness and uncertainty, with individuals who —poor or rich—nourish illusions and suffer the frustrations and indignities of life. His most popular ghost story is about a poor governess who has taken a position in a rich home and is nervously trying to please her employer. No writer has given us a more deeply felt picture of people lost in great cities; or evoked with more power "the bench of desolation"—the drama of human loneliness.

His tales belong to a greater age of leisure than ours. He develops them unhurriedly; he takes his reader step by step into his given situation. There is a fascination in watching him go about his business: he is always precise, always master of his materials, always ready to clear the way and confront his audience. Then he brushes in the detail and his anecdote is told, his picture painted. He has a way of making us hear a number of voices, including his own, and of seeing the world through many eyes. And whether he wears the mask of comedy or of tragedy, we are aware that he is summarizing life, capturing some fragment of it, seeking its essence. And he achieved his intention: his tales "constitute a total having a certain value as observation and testimony." Some, to be sure, are trivial; but the most memorable have become a part of human experience, they have entered into the fabric of our language and our literature, and conveyed to us a sense of how genius can find an undiminished fascination in the episodic, the anecdotal, and the pictorial of the human scene.

## *Chronology of Important Dates*

| | |
|---|---|
| 1843 | Born April 15, No. 21 Washington Place, New York City. |
| 1843-44 | Taken abroad by parents. |
| 1845-55 | Childhood in Albany and New York City. |
| 1855-58 | Attends schools in Geneva, London, Paris and is privately tutored. |
| 1858 | Lives in Newport, R. I. |
| 1859 | At school in Geneva; studies in Bonn. |
| 1860 | At school in Newport. Receives back injury while serving as volunteer fireman; studies art briefly; friendship with John La Farge. |
| 1862-63 | Year at Harvard Law School. |
| 1864 | Family settles in Boston and then in Cambridge. James's first story and early reviews published. |
| 1865 | First story in *Atlantic Monthly.* |
| 1869-70 | Travels in England, France, and Italy. Death of cousin, Minny Temple. |
| 1870 | Back in Cambridge, publishes first novel, *Watch and Ward.* |
| 1872-74 | Travels in Europe, autumn 1872 in Paris, greater part of 1873 in Rome. Begins *Roderick Hudson.* |
| 1874-75 | Tries New York City, writing literary journalism for *Nation.* First three books published: *Transatlantic Sketches, A Passionate Pilgrim,* and *Roderick Hudson.* |
| 1875-76 | Year in Paris with Turgenev, Flaubert, Edmond de Goncourt, Zola, Daudet. Writes *The American.* |
| 1876-77 | Settles in London in Bolton Street. Revisits Paris, Rome. |
| 1878 | "Daisy Miller" establishes his fame on both sides of the Atlantic. *French Poets and Novelists.* |
| 1879-82 | *The Europeans, Washington Square, Confidence, The Portrait of a Lady.* |
| 1882-83 | Revisits America, death of parents. |

| | |
|---|---|
| 1884-86 | Resumes residence in London; sister Alice comes to live near him. Fourteen-volume collection of novels and tales published. |
| 1886 | Takes flat in De Vere Gardens. *The Bostonians. The Princess Casamassima.* |
| 1887 | Long stay in Italy. "The Aspern Papers," *The Reverberator,* "A London Life." Friendship with Constance Fenimore Woolson. |
| 1888 | *Partial Portraits* and various volumes of tales. |
| 1889-90 | *The Tragic Muse.* |
| 1890-91 | "Dramatic years." Seeks to win a place in the theater. Dramatizes *The American,* which has short run. Writes four comedies. |
| 1892 | Death of Alice James. |
| 1894 | Miss Woolson commits suicide in Venice. James journeys to Italy and visits her grave in Rome. |
| 1895 | He is booed at first night of his play *Guy Domville.* Abandons theater. |
| 1897-98 | Settles in Lamb House, Rye, Sussex. Writes "The Turn of the Screw." |
| 1899-1900 | *The Awkward Age. The Sacred Fount.* |
| 1902-1904 | Writes *The Ambassadors, The Wings of the Dove,* and *The Golden Bowl.* |
| 1905 | Revisits United States after twenty-year absence, lectures on Balzac. |
| 1906-1910 | *The American Scene.* Edits selective "New York Edition" published in twenty-four volumes. |
| 1910 | Death of William James. |
| 1913 | Sargent paints his portrait on seventieth birthday. Writes his autobiographies, *A Small Boy and Others, Notes of a Son and Brother.* |
| 1914 | *Notes on Novelists.* Begins war work. |
| 1915 | Becomes British subject. |
| 1916 | Given Order of Merit. Dies February 28 in Chelsea, aged seventy-two years and ten months. Funeral in Chelsea Old Church. Ashes buried in Cambridge (Mass.) cemetery. |

# *Notes on the Editor and Authors*

LEON EDEL, biographer of Henry James, received the 1963 Pulitzer prize as well as the National Book Award for Vols. II and III of his biography. He is also the author of *The Modern Psychological Novel* and *Literary Biography,* and has edited the complete plays and tales of Henry James. He is professor of English at New York University.

JOSEPH CONRAD, Anglo-Polish novelist, was a friend and admirer of Henry James at the turn of the century.

MAX BEERBOHM, wit and caricaturist, served as drama critic of the *Saturday Review,* succeeding Bernard Shaw; among his parodies those best known are of Henry James.

EZRA POUND, American poet and essayist, wrote on Henry James during his early years in England.

EDITH WHARTON, friend and disciple of Henry James, is the author of many novels, of which the best known are *The Age of Innocence, The House of Mirth,* and *Ethan Frome.*

PERCY LUBBOCK, novelist and essayist, edited James's letters in 1920, and wrote *The Craft of Fiction,* one of the seminal studies of modern fictional techniques.

VIRGINIA WOOLF, novelist, knew James when she was a child, and wrote a number of anonymous reviews of his later works for the *Times Literary Supplement.*

T. S. ELIOT has written very little on Henry James but he was among the earliest to estimate Hawthorne's place in James's background, and his own life in London has certain parallels with that of James.

VAN WYCK BROOKS, literary historian, wrote about Henry James not only in the volume devoted to the novelist, but also in his *Makers and Finders* series.

EDMUND WILSON, critic, poet, playwright, and novelist, has written much on James, including the notable study of his "ambiguity," which has often been reprinted.

E. M. FORSTER, novelist, often deals with the work of James when he discusses the art of fiction.

WILLIAM TROY, a distinguished critic of the moderns and of the cinema, left at his death a number of studies of James.

PELHAM EDGAR, who was for many years professor of English at Victoria College, Toronto, was one of the earliest students of the novel form and of James in America.

STEPHEN SPENDER, poet and critic, was one of the most perceptive early critics of Henry James.

GRAHAM GREENE, novelist, has written a number of essays on James and an introduction to the World's Classics edition of *The Portrait of a Lady*.

AUSTIN WARREN, biographer of the elder James, is professor of English at the University of Michigan.

ADELINE TINTNER, a student of iconography, lives in New York.

IRVING HOWE has written books on Faulkner and Sherwood Anderson. He edited the volume on Edith Wharton in the Twentieth Century Views series.

# *Selected Bibliography*

For a complete listing of Henry James's writings see *A Bibliography of Henry James* by Leon Edel and Dan H. Laurence (London: Hart-Davis, 1957; second edition, revised, 1961). This work establishes the priority of editions as between America and England and also lists foreign translations of James's writings.

The "New York Edition" of James's selected novels and tales, containing twelve of his twenty novels and half of his 112 tales, as well as the prefaces James wrote especially for this edition, is being reprinted by Charles Scribner's Sons.

*The Complete Tales of Henry James,* edited by Leon Edel, is being published in twelve volumes by J. B. Lippincott Company.

JAMES'S NOVELS:

*Watch and Ward*
*Roderick Hudson*
*The American*
*The Europeans*
*Confidence*
*Washington Square*
*The Portrait of a Lady*
*The Bostonians*
*The Princess Casamassima*
*The Reverberator*
*The Tragic Muse*
*The Other House*
*The Spoils of Poynton*
*What Maisie Knew*
*The Awkward Age*
*The Sacred Fount*
*The Wings of the Dove*
*The Ambassadors*

*The Golden Bowl*
*The Outcry*

UNFINISHED AND POSTHUMOUS:

*The Ivory Tower*
*The Sense of the Past*

OTHER WRITINGS:

*French Poets and Novelists*
*Hawthorne*
*Partial Portraits*
*Essays in London*
*Notes on Novelists*
*Transatlantic Sketches*
*Portraits of Places*
*A Little Tour in France*
*English Hours*
*The American Scene*
*Italian Hours*
*William Wetmore Story and His Friends* (Biography)
*A Small Boy and Others* (Autobiography)
*Notes of a Son and Brother* (Autobiography)
*The Complete Plays of Henry James* (ed. Edel)

BOOKS ABOUT JAMES:

Anderson, Quentin, *The American Henry James,* 1957.
Beach, Joseph Warren, *The Method of Henry James,* 1918.
Brooks, Van Wyck, *The Pilgrimage of Henry James,* 1925.
Cargill, Oscar, *The Novels of Henry James,* 1961.
Dupee, F. W., *Henry James,* 1951.
Edel, Leon, *Henry James: The Untried Years,* 1953; *The Conquest of London,* 1962; *The Middle Years,* 1962.
Edel, Leon and Gordon N. Ray, *Henry James and H. G. Wells,* 1958.
Edgar, Pelham, *Henry James: Man and Author,* 1927.
Krook, Dorothea, *The Ordeal of Consciousness in Henry James,* 1962.
Leavis, F. R., *The Great Tradition,* 1948.
Matthiessen, F. O., *Henry James: The Major Phase,* 1944.

Matthiessen, F. O. and Kenneth B. Murdock, *The Notebooks o Henry James,* 1947.
Nowell-Smith, Simon, *The Legend of the Master,* 1948.
Poirier, Richard, *The Comic Sense of Henry James,* 1960.
Trilling, Lionel, *The Liberal Imagination,* 1950.
Wegelin, Christof, *The Image of Europe in Henry James,* 1958.
Wilson, Edmund, *The Triple Thinkers,* 1948.
Zabel, Morton Dauwen, *Craft and Character,* 1957.